The Other Side of Memory

The Other Side of Memory

Harry L. Serio

RESOURCE *Publications* • Eugene, Oregon

THE OTHER SIDE OF MEMORY

Copyright © 2022 Harry L. Serio. All rights reserved. Except for brief quotations in critical publications or reviews, no part of this book may be reproduced in any manner without prior written permission from the publisher. Write: Permissions, Wipf and Stock Publishers, 199 W. 8th Ave., Suite 3, Eugene, OR 97401.

Resource Publications
An Imprint of Wipf and Stock Publishers
199 W. 8th Ave., Suite 3
Eugene, OR 97401

www.wipfandstock.com

PAPERBACK ISBN: 978-1-7252-7372-6
HARDCOVER ISBN: 978-1-7252-7373-3
EBOOK ISBN: 978-1-7252-7374-0

VERSION NUMBER 070622

Scripture quotations are from New Revised Standard Version Bible (NRSV), copyright © 1989 National Council of the Churches of Christ in the United States of America. Used by permission. All rights reserved worldwide.

"Lines on a Hope Abandoned" by Clement W. DeChant, copyright © 1952 by The Christian Education Press; copyright renewed 1980 by Alliene DeChant. Permission granted by The Pilgrim Press. All other rights reserved.

Contents

Preface | vii

Rosebud | 1

The Shed—Storehouse of Memories | 6

The House with Nobody in It | 8

Books | 10

Television | 13

Transcending Our Days | 16

Kuan Yin | 19

Sitting Next to Mr. Lincoln | 22

The Lofty Cup of Gambrinus | 25

"Chipping In" | 28

The Color Test | 30

Knuckles | 35

Ghosts of Christmases Past | 38

The Other Side of the Mirror | 42

Memorial Fruitcake | 45

War Stories | 49

Faraway Places with Strange-Sounding Names | 53

Jackson Whites, Gullah Geechees, and Doukhobors | 56

Down by the Old Mill Stream | 61

The High Meadow | 66

Alliene | 68

Tapestry | 72

Synchronicity | 75

It's About Time | 78

You Can't Go Home Again | 83

Plus Ultra | 86

Latin Class | 90

City of David | 93

Ein Yael | 98

The Sound of Emptiness | 104

Holy Ground | 107

Gospel of Grass | 114

Our Soul's Longing | 117

"Your Mother Is Dying" | 120

Thank You | 126

Dover Beach | 129

Celtic Journeys | 131

Anamchara | 134

"What Is Truth?" | 138

The Bag Lady and the Transient | 144

The Last Bell | 147

Being There | 150

Pou Sto | 153

Tell Me Your Story | 156

Bibliography | 161

Preface

"The child is father of the man" is an old saying used by the poet William Wordsworth. All the fragments and experiences of a child determine who he will become.

The people we speak with, the children we play with, the schools we go to, the teachers we learn from, the shows we watch, the books we read, the places we visit, the spiritual mentors and religious beliefs we are exposed to; the lives of others who have intersected with our own—all shape our own lives and help us to become who we are.

How and what we remember guides us through life and our interaction with persons and events. When Anne Sexton said, "It doesn't matter who my father was; it matters who I remember he was," she was in effect saying that perception often becomes the reality.

The other side of memory is the attribution of meaning and significance to the events of our lives. There is purpose in our being and it may take a lifetime to realize it and understand it. In this book I have attempted to make sense of my varied experiences by exploring a few dimensions of my life. My family heritage, my work as a pastor and teacher, and my interest in archaeology, theater, mystical experiences, and more have all contributed to who I have become and have added texture and meaning to my life.

We all need to share our stories, for, collectively, they tell us who we are. Our stories may in some small way answer the question that an old German mother asked when looking out her window at the vastness and complexity of her world, "*Was soll das Alles?*" "What does it all mean?"

We have our own stories to tell, and since we are all part of the same universe and the one mind of God, our individual stories will have meaning to the whole of life.

Rosebud

―

The house on Marne Street in Newark's Ironbound section had been in our family for a hundred years. When my grandparents, Lucas and Natalie, were married, they purchased the small "two-up, two-down" house built in the Frutchey development. It was truly a small house for the husband and wife, one son, and three daughters who lived there. There were only two bedrooms, a living room, and a kitchen, with a toilet and sink in the basement. Later, Lucas would get rid of the coal bin in the cellar and move the kitchen downstairs. A porcelain cookstove would heat the entire house, with the warmth rising through two registers in the first and second floors. As primitive as this sounds, for most immigrants from Europe at the turn of the twentieth century, this was luxury.

Lucas and Natalie had both emigrated from Russia, which was ruled by Tzar Nicholas II at the time. Both were ethnic Germans who lived in communities along the Volga River—Lucas from Saratov and Natalie from Tzaritsyn, which later became Stalingrad and now Volgograd. The Germans had been invited by Catherine the Great, a German princess from Anhalt, to settle in Russia sometime in the latter part of the eighteenth century. Catherine claimed that she wanted to show the indolent Russians how their farms could be made more productive when industrious, hard-working Germans tilled the land.

Lucas Wertz was a Volga German who worked on a farm near his village, but faced years of hardship, and decided to come to America, along with many other Russian Germans. He settled in Newark, where there was a large German population. Many were braumeisters who aided the growth of beer production in the city. Lucas, however, worked at the weavers' trade, but loved his beer. His children and grandchildren learned to appreciate a good brew at Sunday dinners. He later served his country during World War I and was awarded the Victory Medal.

Natalie Grauberger came from an upper-middle-class family. The Graubergers were rather well off. Her father owned a leather goods factory, and was a purveyor of leather boots and other items to the tzar. Natalie sometimes accompanied him to Moscow to deliver his work at the Grand Kremlin Palace.

There were rumblings of revolution in Russia in 1916. Natalie had received an offer of marriage from a Mr. Ellenberger in New Jersey. When she left Russia, she travelled first class with her belongings placed in the finest leather luggage from her father's factory. The voyage through the Black Sea, the Mediterranean, and the Atlantic was not without incident. There were storms that the vessel had to endure, but she said that as a young lady she was comforted by the words of the captain, at whose table she frequently dined. His short lecture on seamanship put her at ease.

When Natalie arrived at the port of New York, she did not need to be processed at Ellis Island like so many millions of other new arrivals, but was met by friends who brought her to Newark. She then learned that the man she was to marry had tired of waiting and had married someone else. Natalie later met Lucas, and they married in 1919 and bought the house on Marne Street.

Richard Wertz was the oldest of the children, and perhaps the most enterprising. After returning from service in the Navy, he and Lucas constructed a tool and die shop in the backyard. As a five-year-old, I helped carry bricks from a demolished factory in the north of Newark. But the shop didn't last long. Richie heard the siren call, and it was "California, here I come," and he headed west to the Tujunga Valley. After working as a butler to the actor Jimmy Cagney, he left to make his fortune in the burgeoning real estate market, and later moved to the Rogue River area of Oregon. Richie and his wife, Barbara, became Jehovah's Witnesses and would return east to attend their conventions in New York. We would have great disputations over biblical interpretations, and I would always be grateful for his sharpening of my skills in resisting the Witnesses when they rang my doorbell. I would tell them that I was in the Jehovah's Witness Protection Program.

Elsie Wertz was the oldest daughter and the most creative. She was an artist, photographer, vocalist, and collector of books. She had a huge volume of Currier and Ives prints that I would often look at and wish to return to the idyllic and pastoral scenes of mid-nineteenth century America. Elsie loved to take Public Service mystery bus trips. She would take me to then obscure places like the Wanaque Reservoir, or Grover Cleveland's birthplace, or some place along the shore. She loved museums, whether to view photographs or paintings or bits of history. The tool and die shop at the rear of the Marne Street house was converted to her studio and darkroom. I was her model for many of the photos she took, including a prize-winning picture of *Little Caballero*, which was my first media appearance. Elsie had a beautiful singing voice and sang in the German choir at St. Stephan's Deutsche Evangelische Kirche, my home church. She recorded with her sisters the folk song "The Butcher Boy."

Dorothea, or Dottie, was a waitress at the Terzis Restaurant in the Jewish Weequahic section of Newark. The restaurant made some of the best cheesecake this side of heaven. Dottie married Frank Rygiel, who served with the Army Rangers during World War II, and lived with us while Frank was fighting in the Pacific. Frank was Polish, and they later moved to a two-room apartment on Mott Street and then to a third-floor flat on Fleming Avenue in the Polish section of the Ironbound. Dottie soon learned to make wonderful Polish meals of pierogis, golabki, and rogal świętomarciński, a poppy seed dessert. The kielbasa and babkas came from Teddy's located next to St. Stephan's Church.

My mother, Matilda, was the youngest of the Wertz family and the first to marry, eloping to Maryland with an Italian pugilist Harry, my father, for whom I was named. Harry was the 1940 Perth Amboy Golden Gloves winner and was later inducted into the New Jersey Boxing Hall of Fame with other illustrious fighters like Jersey Joe Walcott, Mike Tyson and Two-Ton Tony Galento, who had been a sparring partner, and was the only boxer to knock down Joe Louis.

Tillie first worked at Northern Feather Works, sewing sleeping bags for the Army. She would put notes of support and encouragement in the bags, and when found out, her supervisor told her to continue since it aided morale. After the war, she worked for Western Electric and as a lab technician for Bell Labs.

She was a prolific writer of poetry and letters. While much of her correspondence has been saved, almost all of her poetry has been lost. I keep hoping that it will turn up someday. She wrote to her family and her many friends, and she acknowledged every gift and kindness shown to her. She was generous almost to her fault, remembering every birthday, anniversary, and graduation. Her generosity extended to every charity that wrote to her. I don't know how many Native American dream catchers, St. Jude medals, or notepads she accumulated, but she made good use of all the greeting cards she received from Sacred Heart Missions, the Redemptorists, the Columban Fathers, and every Catholic institution that promised to say Mass for her.

Tillie Serio was quite an attractive blue-eyed blonde, a virtual party girl who went out on Saturday nights to the best night clubs. She apparently knew many celebrities, such as Frank Sinatra, Tony Bennett, and other New Jersey–born persons of note. She saved everything, from matchbook covers to swizzle sticks, hundreds of letters, notes, diary entries, and literally thousands of photos. Among her accumulations were the extensive memorabilia of my brother, Robert, who died young, and a large collection of Uncle Emilio's cards and artwork.

After Tillie's passing at the age of almost ninety-three, we began the process of emptying out her house on Marne Street. Saving what we could, the rest was piled up at the curb to be picked over by the neighbors and passersby, and then hauled away. Who knew what memories were discarded?

I thought of the 1941 classic film *Citizen Kane*. You may remember the opening scene of the fog-shrouded castle on the hill, the home of Charles Foster Kane, a titan of a newspaper empire, like William Randolph Hearst. Within moments, Kane is dead, uttering the word "Rosebud" as he slips into eternity and lets fall from his hands a snow globe. The newspaper that he had owned, the *New York Inquirer*, tries desperately to understand the meaning of his last word.

As the workmen are crating the works of art and packaging that which can be sold, they are also burning the trivial accumulations of Kane's lifetime. A reporter ponders the meaning of Kane's last word, "Rosebud," and says, "Perhaps Rosebud was something he couldn't get or something he lost. Anyway, it wouldn't have explained anything. I don't think any word can explain a man's life. No, I guess Rosebud is just a piece in a jigsaw puzzle." The final image is that of a little sled being thrown into a fire with the name "Rosebud" on it.

We are led to reflect on the meaning of a person's life, of our life, when at the time of our death all that we have accumulated, all that we have achieved, all that we have done fades into the oblivion of the past. Joy Ufema, a pioneer in the care of the dying, once said that when you are on your death bed, the only thing you will have left will be your memories, so make sure that they are good ones. It's good advice since the experience of living is all that will transcend this life. Charles Foster Kane had only the memory of a lost childhood, happiness, and innocence, represented in the relic of his youth now consigned to the flames.

Rosebud reminds us that the pursuit of things is the pursuit of vapor and illusion. Rosebud represents not only the memory of what has eluded us, but that which is implanted in our souls from before we were born, and which in the course of living we forget about—until some major tragedy awakens us and shocks us back to our true goal.

In fact, the entirety of the film *Citizen Kane* might be Kane's own dreamed recollections in the last moment before his death—his life flashing before his, and our, eyes. It is said that at the time of our death the whole of our life appears before us as a gestalt, a single entity in which we are able, finally, to grasp the entire meaning of our existence before the film runs off the projector and flaps endlessly on the reel. We are then left in the dark to consider what we have seen and wishing we could have played some of the scenes differently.

C. S. Lewis once said, "The doors of hell are locked from the inside." I think that's true. We hold within ourselves the power to determine where we will spend eternity by our perceptions and the actions we take on the basis of those perceptions. We ourselves are heaven and hell, and it is our choice.

When I think back to my family, my parents, my aunts and uncles, my grandparents, and all the memories of our lives together, and of all that has been forgotten, I know deep in my very being that nothing is ever lost, but all is retained in the heart of God and affects us into eternity.

The Shed—Storehouse of Memories

As early as I can remember, there was a small structure in the rear of our yard on Marne Street. When my grandparents bought the four-room house early in the twentieth century, it soon became too small. The first expansion was to move the kitchen to the basement, which it shared with the coal storage bin. When carrying the ashes out to the ash can became too much of a chore, Lucas Wertz went to kerosene heat. Since it was too dangerous to keep a fifty-five-gallon drum near the kitchen, a small shed was built to house the tank.

When Uncle Richie returned from the Navy after the Second World War, he and Lucas decided to open a tool and die shop to make precision parts for the growing manufacturing industries in the area. There were tables with lathes and other cutting devices and all manner of tools. It didn't last very long. When Richie took off for California, Elsie took over the shed for her photography studio, complete with a posing area and a darkroom. A photo enlarger replaced the lathe, and trays for developing and fixing, as well as the chemicals, were placed on the shelves. When Elsie got married, it was all left behind.

The shed now became a storage area. After my parents' divorce and Lucas's death, we moved from our Monroe Street apartment to live on Marne Street with Natalie. The old furniture was stored in the shed to make room for the newer furniture that we brought with us. Here also was the detritus of an earlier life. Our first television was there, the small thirteen-inch Philco screen in a large stand-up console. Here also was the cathedral-type radio that Lucas and Natalie would listen to each night. It was not only entertainment, but a tool of history. Lucas heard President Roosevelt announce the "Day of Infamy" when Pearl Harbor was bombed, and the Fireside Chats of the president that brought encouragement and comfort during the Great Depression and the World War. On the shelf were kerosene lanterns that were used at blackouts during the war. FDR was greatly admired and a metal plate with his initials was on the wall, as was a poster of Harry Truman, whom folks said looked a lot like Lucas Wertz.

I still have some of the old tools from my grandfather's workbench: wood-handled screwdrivers, brace and bits for drilling, part of a railroad iron used as an anvil, and other miscellaneous items now obsolete and, in some cases, of unknown usage.

Milton Lis was the president of Teamsters Local 478, but he liked to make money on the side by buying out bankrupt businesses and reselling the office equipment. I helped on one occasion and Milton allowed me to appropriate an old desk and chair, which I installed in a corner of the shed. This became my office, where I would do my homework, write stories, and, as a Boy Scout patrol leader, hold meetings and plan events for my patrol. More importantly, it was my space, a place to be apart from the normal noise of the family and the "do this" demands of my mother and grandmother. Surrounded by my books, and Elsie's left-behind classics, I could enter my own world and travel to times and places I could only dream about.

The shed became a storehouse for many memories, but as time passed much of it was put out for trash, and today would fetch much in the antiques market. However, what we value, what we remember, shapes our future, and we build our lives on what we have left behind.

The dominant genre today for young people is fantasy, in film, video games, graphic novels, and books. It provides escape from our present reality. Even as adults, we still need a place apart, a respite from the daily cares or monotonous routines—a shed, an alternate universe, a place to cultivate a different form of existence or perspective on life.

Jesus said that the kingdom of God is within you. We apprehend the Divine within our own consciousness. As Jesus did that by going to a lonely place apart from the crowds—a wilderness, a mountaintop, a lake, a garden—we can do the same. It may be a special place in our home, a tree in a park, a morning watch spot at camp, a church, a shed. It is a place where we can think our thoughts, free of distraction, of interruption.

I had many places in my life when God seemed to draw closer. My shed of memories was only the beginning.

The House with Nobody in It

The house is empty now. I sit alone remembering the way it was. The furniture is now gone. Uncle Emilio's paintings have been taken down. Family photos are packed away. Nothing remains but bare walls and the faint echoes of memories.

With my mother Tillie's passing, the hundred-year history of our family on Marne Street has ended. We now await the sale to new owners seeking an ideal location in the New York metropolitan area who are willing to pay much more than the four-room house is worth, simply because of its location.

I can still hear the laughter of family gatherings, the sounds of play when brothers and cousins come together, the old radio with my grandmother Natalie's "stories" of *Stella Dallas* and *Mary Noble, Backstage Wife*, and grandfather Lucas's *The Lone Ranger* and *The Shadow*. The small dining room was often crammed with relatives and friends, sitting shoulder to shoulder around the table laden with elaborate and exotic foods. Tillie would spend hours preparing these magnificent repasts—but not by hovering over a stove. There were Italian pastries, luscious cheesecake and blintzes from the Weequahic Diner, galumkis and babka from Teddy's, and an assorted mixture of German, Italian, Russian, Polish, Jewish, and Greek delicacies.

In one corner of the room was a large cart of bottles of expensive wines and liqueurs. Tillie seldom bought a bottle, nor did she consume much of it, except for an occasional taste or sampling. The alcohol were gifts from friends at Christmas when the only presents they could think of was Courvoisier, Remy Martin, or Johnny Walker Blue. Tillie did bring back bottles of rum when she returned from her condo in Isla Verde, Puerto Rico. Most likely, they were her gifts to her friends and relatives.

Although the dining room was the place of large gatherings, of good memories and gaiety, it was also a room of sadness. It was here that Lucas Wertz died of stomach cancer in 1954. He had never wanted anyone to make a fuss over him. When Tillie bought him a sweater for his birthday, he said to her, "Why are you doing this? I'm dying." Mom replied, "You're not dead yet. So enjoy it."

Tillie was a poet, and a good one. Her poems were gathered in an old canvas-covered loose-leaf binder. As much as I have scoured the old house, I have not been able to find it. Such a loss. She not only loved writing poetry; she memorized much of it and would quote many of the poems to us. In particular, I remember her reciting Joyce Kilmer's poem "The House with Nobody in It." Kilmer was a New Jersey poet, killed in action during World War I. He is most noted for his poem "Trees." Now sitting in the empty house, I remember one verse that Mom loved to recite:

> But a house that has done what a house should do,
> a house that has sheltered life,
> That has put its loving wooden arms around a man and his wife,
> A house that has echoed a baby's laugh and held up his stumbling feet,
> Is the saddest sight, when it's left alone, that ever your eyes could meet.

Kilmer also wrote:

> I know this house isn't haunted, and I wish it were, I do;
> For it wouldn't be so lonely if it had a ghost or two.

The house on Marne Street will have its ghosts, if only in the memory of those who enjoyed their company in life and who learned from their wisdom, and grew to be the persons they have become.

Books

Growing up in an old-world neighborhood, there might be some who would consider my family poor. We did not live in poverty. We had the essentials of life and did not lack for food, clothing, and shelter. During World War II, when I didn't like what was on my dinner plate, I was constantly reminded of the starving masses in Europe and victims of war in Asia. We always seemed to have enough.

We weren't rich by any means. One of my earliest fundraising enterprises was to travel the neighborhood in search of bottles that I could cash in for the deposits. It was enough to provide me with pocket money. Delivering newspapers also supplemented my income.

The family was careful with its meager income. I would walk the nine blocks to the Nabisco bakery factory to buy bread for ten cents after the delivery trucks returned with their leftovers. The grocery store around the corner kept a tab that was like an early version of the credit card. Both the Weiss sisters and mother ran a one-room store from their home on Magazine Street, and Sid had a larger market on Adams Street. Both issued little memo-type books where they would write down your purchase. Some stores also gave you Green Stamps. Sid had boys who would deliver your groceries. My mother would be embarrassed when there was a note that the tab was getting too large, and she would have to remind my father on his occasional visits to pay the bill.

We may have been poor in other material things, but we were rich in books. The used book store near the Nabisco bakery was a good source for hardbound classics, but I also possessed a magnificent library of comic books, particularly the Dell and Marvel action characters. Considering their value today, I am sorry I gave up that early investment. However, I still have an almost complete collection of the early *Classics Illustrated*, and my reading of the novels by Dickens, Dumas, Stevenson, and others inspired me to read the original texts. I could spend hours at the branch library.

The church was my other place of refuge. When Billy Graham had his New York Crusade at Madison Square Garden, St. Stephan's Church sponsored a bus trip. I went, and I made the mistake of responding to Billy's invitation to be "saved." The Crusade passed by contact information to a fundamentalist group known as Hi-BA, or High School Born-Againers. I joined the group and they encouraged us to carry our Bibles to school so that we could "witness" to our classmates.

John Venlet, the group's leader, would pick me up after school to attend their meetings. When he was putting my books in his car one day, he noticed that I was reading John Steinbeck's *The Grapes of Wrath*. He commented that it was a "bad" book and that I shouldn't be reading such "trash." That was the end of my excursion into far-right Christianity. I now redefined the meaning of being "saved" as being rescued from those who would prohibit what I read and what I thought.

I found myself drawn to some of the writers of the Southern Renaissance. I wasn't that interested in the culture of the South, but writers such as William Faulkner, Thomas Wolfe, Flannery O'Connor, Margaret Mitchell, Harper Lee, Zora Neale Hurston, and others were too good to ignore. I did my master's thesis on the works of Tennessee Williams. Two other writers that resonated with me were F. Scott Fitzgerald and Ernest Hemingway.

Tennessee Williams is a poet of our times. His plays reflected the world as he saw it. Williams has one major theme and all his plays are expressions of its various aspects: hell is the world we live in, made by us, and the only way to survive is to conform to the world's demands. The words that describe this world and the people in it are a dreary lot: decadence, despair, forsakenness, loneliness, misunderstanding, illusions, sexuality, hopelessness, disintegration. The tragedy of human life is not something that is arbitrarily injected into the scheme of things by some outside force. Tragedy and suffering are made by humans, a natural part of society that results whenever persons encounter one another. It may arise out of a person's inability to relate or communicate with another person. It may result from a person's failure to escape the world of reality. It may come with the passage of time and the longing for the past when life seemed somewhat rosier.

The characters of Tennessee Williams are tragic characters in tragic situations. They are defeated persons who are forced to live in this world against their will or commit suicide to escape. The only wholesome characters are those who recognize the human situation for what it is and conform to it. Hell is bearable only if you are a part of it. If you seek to escape it through illusory ideals, it only engulfs and destroys you. The world of Tennessee Williams is one of cold reality, devoid of transcendent idealism and elusory hopes.

Tennessee Williams described a world that many experienced in the mid-twentieth century. While in seminary, I wrote a paper that sought to address only a few of the expressions of secular damnation, particularly the misunderstanding between individuals that causes loneliness and despair; Williams's obsession with sexuality; the passage of time as it has affected several characters; the defeat of idealism by realism or a flight into fantasy; and finally, personal atonement in which the idealist is devoured and cannibalized by an evil and depraved world.

Reading was not just an escape from my own story, but a vicarious participation in the lives of others. Though fictitious, the stories I read provided insight into the human comedy as well as the human tragedy. It also provided the hope that we can all emerge into a better world and find our own fulfillment and reason for being.

Television

In a modern paraphrase of the book of Proverbs, it has been said that "where there is no television, the people perish." For those born BC (before computers), television was from its earliest days a most transforming invention and had great impact upon American culture. It was not only an electronic babysitter, but a tool for social gathering and information about what was happening in remote parts of the planet.

Our first television was a large box that occupied a central part of the living room. The 1947 Philco TV had a thirteen-inch screen, about the size of a modern iPad, and you had to sit really close to watch the grainy figures and tolerate the various forms of distortion that the early sets were prone to.

I had just entered first grade when the television arrived, but it wasn't long before it became addictive. I would run home to watch *The Howdy Doody Show* with Buffalo Bob and the inane cast of characters that included Dilly Dally, Flubadub, Mr. Bluster, and the beautiful Native American Princess SummerFall WinterSpring. And of course there was the clown Clarabell, played by the future Captain Kangaroo, Bob Keeshan, who would wreak havoc with his seltzer bottle. *Kukla, Fran and Ollie* came next, but by that time I was tiring of adults who talked to puppets, and the cartoons featuring Farmer Brown and Al Falfa were just too ridiculous.

Lessons in science were brought by *Mr. Wizard*, who prompted me to create my own chemistry lab in the basement, and by *Captain Video* and *Tom Corbett, Space Cadet*, who motivated me to consider a career in astrophysics and interstellar law enforcement. It was the Westerns that were the most ubiquitous and I knew all of the cowboys, even winning a naming contest with my Uncle Bones. The problem with these one-hour "shoot-'em-ups" was that they taught young minds that most problems could be resolved with a gun, and that horses were to be loved more than beautiful women. When our television failed to work one day, Uncle Bones said that we had to call the TV repairman to clean out all the dead cowboys that were clogging up the tubes.

The forties and fifties were also the time of the singing cowboy. Roy Rogers and Gene Autry were the most famous and I got to shake hands with both of them. A friend of my father was Jimmie Dale, who lived around the corner on Lafayette Street. He had his own band, Pride of the Prairies, and would perform at various gigs in the city and occasionally on WAAT's *Home Town Frolics*, hosted by Don Larkin, who played "hillbilly" music, which he once said he never liked. Jimmie performed live on the show and once dedicated his rendition of "Wabash Cannonball" to me. I delighted in hearing my name mentioned on air, but the song I had requested was Autry's "That Little Kid Sister of Mine." It was hard to imagine Jimmie as a cowboy. I never saw him riding a horse down Lafayette Street in Newark.

My father was a professional boxer, so it was inevitable that he would invite all his friends over for the Friday night fights. I didn't mind it since on Saturday morning I got to collect all the bottles to be returned for the deposit as well as all the loose change in the sofa and chairs.

Television was an important part of growing up, but it was a novelty that would soon wear off. My grandparents were still addicted to the old radio shows. Grandma Wertz would stop whatever she was doing to tune in to what she called "my story." Before she would begin dinner, she had to listen to *Stella Dallas* and *Mary Noble, Backstage Wife*. When her husband, Lucas, would come home after working at the weavers' trade, he would take down his tobacco tin, roll up a cigarette, and listen to *The Lone Ranger* and *The Shadow*. Like the Shadow, I sometimes got to learn "what evil lurks in the hearts and minds of men." And returning to those thrilling days of yesteryear when the Lone Ranger rides again, the strains of Rossini's "William Tell Overture" would cause me to wonder whatever happened to my six-shooter cap pistol.

It wasn't long before my addiction soon morphed to the printed page and books supplanted the noise of the tube. Our lives are often shaped by what we subject ourselves to. There is no doubt that the television has shaped our culture. Just as film reflects who we are, it also influences what we have become. I often wonder if we have become more violent as a society because of our exposure to violence on radio and television as a means of resolving problems. Unfortunately the long history of the human species is replete with war, destruction, murder, and mayhem. Television has just become another mirror to the human soul. But thankfully it has also reflected that which is ennobling and aspiring, and that which challenges us to become better than we are.

Transcending Our Days

When my nephew was cleaning out his father's house after his death, he came across a box of photographs, which he sent to us. Here were hundreds of snapshots tossed into an old shoebox, the events of a lifetime accumulated over the years: Stuart's first haircut, Tasha opening a Christmas present, Matthew's first encounter with a wave at the shore. Here they were, fragments of memories preserved in a moment frozen in time.

Also in the box were other photos, much older, snapshots of experiences that no one living can remember. They must have been important at the time, but are now almost useless, because we can't attribute any meaning to them. Perhaps another generation will look at our pictures the way we look at the faces that peer at us from the nineteenth century and will wonder who they were, what their names were, what their lives were like, what their hopes and dreams were.

What will happen to the events of our own lives? Will they too be gone forever when we who remember them are gone? Will we too a hundred years from now be nothing more than a faded photograph, a dim memory in a descendant's faltering recollection? It's hard to imagine that each one of us will one day be an ancestor.

I attended a meeting at Mensch Mill, the camp of our church, which was created by Fred Wentzel, the former pastor of the church I served. They had a display of group photographs going back to the beginning of the camp experience. Here were people I had known who are long gone, or who are now in their senior years. Here were Mary Ann and me, and two other clergy couples that summer we first met. Here were the little kids that grew up to be pastors and teachers, doctors, lawyers, and housewives.

A group of us gathered about the table trying to identify these pictures and wondering what became of people whom we knew for only a week or two in a summer a long time ago.

It is strange and wonderful how we move in and out of each other's lives, sometimes very briefly, but we are changed forever because of one moment in time. Those moments are not lost. The photographs may fade, but the people and events, and all the memories of every person who has ever lived, continue forever in the mind of God. Each fragment of our lives shapes in some small way the history of the human race and we can never know what impact we will have on the future.

We are a pilgrim people. We are here for a moment and then we are gone. From birth until death, we are simply passing through this world. Nothing in this life is forever. How we would love to preserve the days of our youth and speak once more to friends and family long gone. We would like to capture magical moments in the lives of our children and hold on to them, but life is a moving stream. As Shakespeare's Macbeth said,

> Life's but a walking shadow, a poor player,
> That struts and frets his hour upon the stage,
> And then is heard no more. It is a tale
> Told by an idiot, full of sound and fury,
> Signifying nothing.[1]

That is the value of photographs. They freeze time for a moment and allow us to hold on to the past just a little longer. But the experience is gone like a vaper and reminds us of the importance of making every moment count. Because life passes so quickly, we must focus on the things that really do matter.

My mother lived into her nineties. When she passed on, I gathered the remnants of her life. In addition to the many large boxes of photos, there were her writings, bits of poetry, diaristic notes of her mundane existence. In her younger days, she was something of a party girl, spending Friday and Saturday nights at clubs, parties, and cabarets, with an assortment of people—the famous, the infamous, the ordinary. Here were allusions to her brief connections to Tony Bennett, Frank Sinatra, Lucille Ball, and others. How well she knew them I will never know, since she seldom spoke of them.

What interested me was the fact that she had saved the Christmas greeting cards and other cards and postcards that she had received over

---

1. *Macbeth*, act 5, scene 5.

the years. In many of the cards were the trivia of the lives of her friends and the strong sentiments of enduring friendship. Relationships were most important to her.

Our lives are not about things, but about relationships. The material things that we spend our money on are but a moment's sunlight, and then they are gone. The writing on the paper and cards will fade away, but the meaning behind the words will endure forever. There is only one thing that lasts and transcends our existence and that is the love that we share for each other. When we care for others in the way that God cares for us, we are participating in the very nature of God and living into eternity.

Kuan Yin

Emilio Serio's painting of Kuan Yin hung on the wall just inside the door to remind anyone leaving his house of the qualities of mercy and forgiveness. It was also an indication of his own sensitivity, which was evident in his work. Art critics have also noted this.

Kuan Yin is the Chinese bodhisattva whose name means "one who perceives the sounds of the world," or "one who senses the world's lamentations." Jesuit missionaries referred to her as the "goddess of mercy and compassion," which are important attributes in attaining Buddhahood, which is the meaning of a bodhisattva. She is one who listens and who hears the cries of pain and suffering with compassion. Listening to one another with sensitivity to their situation helps to bring about healing.

It is unfortunate that in our world today we tend to become insensitive and immune when we hear each day the news of mass murders, sexual assaults and killings, deaths from COVID, wars and conflagrations, the plight of refugees and immigrants, and the thousands of stories of heartache and pain in families fragmented by misunderstandings and hatred.

Compassion and forgiveness seem to have been replaced by heartlessness and retribution in the governments of this world and in individuals. One wonders if Adolf Hitler would have come to power had the Allies, after the First World War, been more compassionate in victory instead of inflicting oppressive burdens on their defeated adversaries.

According to the prophet Jeremiah, God said to Israel and Judah, "I will forgive their iniquity, and I will remember their sin no more" (31:34). The writer of the Letter to the Hebrews cites these same words (10:12) to assure us that the God that we believe in is not a God of vengeance that pursues us like the Furies of Greek mythology. In the same way, when we are aggrieved, we do not forget the pain inflicted on us, but we learn from it so that we do not hurt others. Forgiveness is not forgetting, but reaching beyond and bestowing grace upon those who have caused our pain.

Native American cultures are so varied in their many expressions across the North American continent, but many of them recognize a Great Spirit (in Algonquin, *Gitche Manitou*) who pervades everything and binds all things together. The Lakota name *Wakȟáŋ Tȟáŋka* means the same thing, or "Great Mystery," and represents the sacred in all things.

Some tribes have ceremonies of forgiveness in which the Great Spirit is invoked to bring healing, not only of fragmented bodies, but of fragmented relationships. In 2016 representatives of a thousand tribes came together with White Americans who sought forgiveness for all the broken treaties, massacres, seizure of tribal lands, misappropriation of mineral rights, desecration of sacred sites, obliteration of tribal culture, and other atrocities, especially against women and children. The sounds of the pain of the world were heard and mercy was extended through the Great Spirit that binds all persons together. This was represented in the sounds of drumming and chanting, which many tribes regard as communication with the Divine. The ceremonial dances were acting out ritually that which is to be desired.

As the Buddhist deity of mercy and compassion who is sensitive to the sounds of the world, Kuan Yin can be seen as an example of the commonality of all the world's religions. To the People of the Book, namely, Jews, Christians, and Sabians (Islam), sound is the first creation of God, since God speaks all things into existence. Hindus believe that "Om" is the sacred sound that represents ultimate reality and the totality of consciousness and all that is.

On my travels through Europe, I would try to enter a church when the monks were observing the Divine Office, usually the canonical hours of None or Vespers in late afternoon or early evening. Finding a quiet spot apart from the tourists, I would listen to the sacred sounds of the monk's chanting. The transcendent sounds would lift me to another state of being where I was in communion with the Divine.

Kuan Yin and Jesus both represent the need for a forgiving heart. It is not just the extension of love to those who have wounded us, but it is also the forgiving of oneself, for what we have done in the past that continues to burden us. Forgiveness is a process of healing that enables us to move on. It is also essential for learning the lessons that life would teach us. When

Jesus prayed to God from the cross and said, "Father, forgive; for they do not know what they are doing" (Luke 23:34), he was acknowledging that humans are still in a state of becoming and have much to learn.

When I look at the painting of Kuan Yin, my thoughts turn to the loving God of my faith, who hears the pain of the world and the cries for healing, and, in the penultimate conclusion, grants forgiveness to all and reconciliation to the God of All That Is.

Sitting Next to Mr. Lincoln

To a child living in the melting pot of many ethnicities, the name of Gutzon Borglum was still strange.

I had heard of Borglum and his incredible feat of carving four presidential heads out of the granite of Mt. Rushmore in South Dakota. We learned about him in Mrs. Wolfe's fifth-grade class. She had taken one of those teacher trips out West, and in September posted her snapshots on the bulletin board as if playing her trump card in the usual essay assignment of what I did on my summer vacation. We sat there fascinated and bored by her statistics of how long it took to carve the sculpture and how much stone had to be cut away. When she spoke of Gutzon Borglum, the name seemed to roll off her tongue while tying ours in knots. I didn't know it then, but the famous sculptor had a significant tie to my city.

Borglum, a Danish Mormon, child of a polygamous marriage and a member of the Ku Klux Klan, suffered from delusions of grandeur and Attention-Deficit/Hyperactivity Disorder. He had trouble completing any project he undertook, but he had no difficulty charming advance payments from those who commissioned his work, especially if they were women. He had promised that he would complete the Mount Rushmore Memorial in a year, but it ended up being a fourteen-year project, with only six and a half years of actual work. Borglum died in 1941 before finishing the work and left it to his son, Lincoln, to oversee its completion.

I never much cared for artists that work with jackhammers and dynamite, or for that matter, artists who drive over massive canvases in Jeeps with paint-laden tires. However, Borglum was noted for other works.

My grandmother, Natalie, had to go to the Hall of Records in Newark, which was located in back of the imposing Essex County Courthouse at the confluence of Springfield and South Orange Avenues. Early childhood, like old age, consists of people taking you where you don't want to go, and Natalie dragged me everywhere.

When we got off the bus in front of the courthouse, I first saw the tall man seated on a bench at the base of the steps. When I noticed the stovepipe hat next to him, I knew immediately that the metal man was Abraham Lincoln. I ran over to look at him and then at the mountain of steps awaiting our ascent. "You go," I said to my grandmother, "I'll wait here."

I was surprised that she agreed. Perhaps she thought that no one would harm a nine-year-old boy sitting next to Mr. Lincoln. Every kid who ever wanted to meet a real live president had to be satisfied with sitting next to Abraham Lincoln and getting their picture snapped with the Great Emancipator. I wonder if I still exist in the pictures of some unknown tourist with a Kodak Brownie.

Gutzon Borglum made the Lincoln statue in 1911. He also made the massive and busy *Wars of America* statue in Military Park. It is a mess of frightened horses, loose cannons, men with guns, struggling to achieve some unknown and unportrayed objective. I suppose that would typify the American dream, but at least the statuary was big enough to be a rendezvous point for shoppers.

I loved Abraham Lincoln. Of course I had heard the stories in my fourth-grade class of how Lincoln had freed the slaves and preserved the union of a divided nation. I saw many images of Lincoln in the pages of Aunt Elsie's massive Currier and Ives book of lithographs, including his assassination by John Wilkes Booth. What fascinated me, however, were the ghost stories. The spectral president was seen by Queen Wilhelmina of the Netherlands, who promptly fainted when she answered his knock at the door. Other residents of the White House also reported seeing the ghost or feeling Lincoln's presence, including Theodore Roosevelt, Grace Coolidge, Winston Churchill, and Lyndon Johnson.

Lincoln himself reported several paranormal events, including a premonition of his death a few days before. He told his friend and former law partner, Ward Hill Lamon, of his precognitive dream. His wife, Mary Todd Lincoln, was interested in spiritualism and the president attended two of the seances that were held in the White House.

These stories would come later, but I remember the strange feelings I had sitting next to Mr. Lincoln that somehow he knew I was there, who I was, and what I would become.

Until recently, I never did come close to a sitting president, except when Harry Truman visited Newark while campaigning for Adlai Stevenson. They had dismissed the children from school so that we could welcome the leader of our country to our fair city, and in 1952 Newark was still fair before its rating would plummet in the following decade. As far as I can remember, Newark had been heavily Democratic, so it was natural for Truman to come and try to get out the vote.

The day was bitterly cold and I sought a vantage point from which I might catch a glimpse of our leader. It was at the top of the steps of city hall. "What a great spot," I thought, imagining the president striding up the steps with his entourage while a military band played "Hail to the Chief," and I would thrust my hand out for him to shake while trying to think of a few appropriate words. "Give 'em hell, Harry" didn't seem quite appropriate.

But it never happened. The presidential motorcade wound its way under the city hall steps to the lower and more protected doors. The best I could do was to lean over the marble wall and peer down. Fortunately, Truman was in an open convertible in the back seat wearing a gray overcoat, bundled against the weather. I could have dropped my notebook in his lap.

It was many years later that I stood in the bitter cold waiting to be admitted to the Kutztown University field house to hear President Bill Clinton. His words were not that memorable, nor was the occasion historic, and my presence was just a drop in the flow of American history. But nevertheless, the thousands of experiences and accumulated memories have added to my world perspective and helped shape who I have become. And the meaning of that is yet to be determined.

The Lofty Cup of Gambrinus

The Ironbound neighborhood in which I lived was home to two of Newark's many breweries. Some sources list as many as fifty-seven breweries in this city founded by New England Puritans, who established a strict theocracy. They paid the local Native American tribe with some trinkets, weapons of war, and four barrels of beer. It seems that beer was present at Newark's creation and became one of the cornerstones of its rise to greatness.

Ballantine Brewing Company was several blocks away from where I lived, founded by Peter Ballantine, a Scotsman, and constructed along the banks of the Passaic River at a time when its water was much more potable. His company, at its peak, was the third largest brewery in America, and one of Newark's biggest employers.

But it was the Hensler brewery, three blocks away from where I lived, that represented the true Germanic culture of the neighborhood. Beer was an essential ingredient in the diet of the German American who inhabited the "Dutch Neck" section of city, later referred to as "Down Neck." Almost every intersection had a mom-and-pop grocery store on one corner and a tavern on another. The taverns and the churches were the social gathering places and beer was present at both. It was no wonder that Joseph Hensler endowed the windows and artwork of St. Stephan's Church, which many of his employees attended and which was reputedly founded when the local Presbyterian church adopted a strict temperance policy. Congregations are established for many reasons, but not many in order to have beer at church gatherings.

Old World customs were brought to the New. The Shady Grove Bier Garten at Jabez Street and New York Avenue was typical with its long tables,

German cuisine, and oompah band, which seemed to constantly play "*Ach, du lieber, Augustin.*" I later learned the origin of this Viennese folk song about a balladeer named Marx Augustin, who got drunk and fell asleep in the gutter on his way home from the beer garden. Since it was during Plague years, the night watch presumed that he was dead and tossed him and his bagpipe into a mass grave. When he awoke, he was unable to get out and started to play his pipes until he was rescued. He later composed the popular drinking song in 1679.

In the late forties beer was still being delivered to the local taverns by horse-drawn wagons. I would watch as the deliveryman stopped at a tavern, tossed down a thick hemp mat, and proceeded to bounce the steel kegs to his assistant. It was done so expeditiously that it seemed like performance art.

The Hensler brewery was on my way to Wilson Avenue School and I would watch the horses and wagons enter the courtyard at the brewery. Horses in the city were not uncommon. Wagons would come down Marne Street almost every day. There was the farmer with his vegetable and fruit produce, the soft pretzel man, the rag man, and others. Nostalgic reverie brings back those idyllic, easygoing, quiet days with fewer automobiles, but how soon we forgot dodging horse manure in the street.

My path to school would take me under the massive statue of Gambrinus who held aloft a tankard of ale. Gambrinus was a mythical German king who became the iconic symbol for breweries and the good life associated with conviviality. There was a local superstition that one should not pass under the statue of the Beer King lest he pour his brew upon you and you would reek of beer as you went to class.

The Germanic brews still evoke the memories of family dinners and friends long gone, but I prefer a more theological approach. While at Mansfield College in Oxford, I visited the Turf Tavern. This malthouse has been serving students since 1381. One night I had a deep and lengthy discourse on theodicy with some British students. It was 1965 and civil rights and Vietnam were topics for discussion, as well as the recent Auschwitz trials in Frankfurt. How could we explain why a loving God would permit such evils to exist in our world? While Martin Luther could give birth to the Protestant Reformation drafting his Ninety-Five Theses in the outhouse, it was in the alehouse that his greatest discourses and sermons had their birth. Perhaps A.E. Housman was right when he said that "malt does more than Milton can to justify God's ways to man."

Nevertheless, good beer, like good theology, must be used in moderation. There is much virtue in the Greek concept of *sophrosyne* as exemplified by Heraclitus and Plato. Wisdom will come in its own time and when the student is ready, the teacher will appear. The Puritan fathers who founded my city with four barrels of beer, the German braumeisters who created a church and a community, and the culture that enabled the *joie de vivre* and fostered some occasional serious philosophical thinking in the local pubs were all part of a process that is still unfolding.

While serving a church in Berks County, Pennsylvania, I began a series called Spirit on Tap. We began meeting in a local tavern, like Martin Luther, but later, as attendance increased, we moved to the large DoubleTree Hotel in Reading. Spirit on Tap is an open forum for faith exploration, theological reflection, and an opportunity to discuss contemporary issues as they impact one's spiritual life and growth. The format is a presentation by noted theologians and persons with expertise in a particular field, followed by an open discussion with shared opinions, comments, or questions. And of course, beer is available.

"Chipping In"

My first lessons in investments, shares, and fractions came underneath the corner streetlamp at Monroe and Elm Streets. The usual neighborhood gang would meet on a summer evening to discuss the comparative merits of Mickey Mantle, Duke Snider, and Willie Mays and other topics of interest to young boys. Of course, there were only two topics of interest: baseball and girls—in that order.

We came from different backgrounds and had different personalities. There was Angelo Santino, a short Italian kid with a fiery temper who was a master at the art of seduction and con artistry, and would pick a fight with you if you got so close to him that you had to look down at him. He was sensitive about his size and you had to be very careful about what you said. Midget baseball would really set him off.

Poncho, whose real name was Jose Berenger, was Mexican (or was he Puerto Rican?—he would never tell), an affable, rotund fellow who exaggerated his accent to be funny, and he was always funny. He usually carried a stick or a knife or something to hit you with, but he never did. He was a good *compadre*.

Tommy was the good kid, well-mannered, polite, soft-spoken, and very gracious. In a neighborhood of takers, Tommy was a giver. He wasn't from around our streets; I think he lived over in East Newark somewhere. But his uncle hung out at the Elm Street Club and he would bring Tommy with him.

Big Joe was older than the others and often threw his weight around. If you crossed him in any way, he would knock you over and sit on you. He loved to tell stories about the bull fights he had seen in Spain, but nobody was interested. They didn't believe him anyway.

Sal was the skinny Italian who loved baseball, but was always too sick to play in the Saturday games at Independence Park. That didn't stop him from carrying a baseball and glove all the time.

We played together and we fought together—and sometimes we ate together. That is how I learned about fractions. There was a ritual that occurred about once a week known as "chipping in." Someone would say "Let's chip in and buy a pie." The pie, of course, was a pizza pie. These were the days before Pizza Hut and Domino's, when there were very few restaurants that had large pizza ovens. But Santa Lucia's on Jefferson Street did.

We each chipped in whatever we had, and the amount we chipped in determined how big a slice we would get. When the money was collected, we would send two of the guys to Santa Lucia's to order the pizza. They had detailed instructions as to how it was to be cut—sometimes diagramed on paper. We tried to be fair.

When Poncho and Sal told the old man how we wanted the pie cut—nine slices with two pieces slightly bigger than the others—he would say, "Getta outta here! Whatta you think I am—a college professor?" He would take the pie, put it into a box, and say to Poncho, "Here, take a dis. You cutta the way you want."

Poncho and Sal brought the pizza to us and when we opened the box, expecting to find wedge-shaped slices, we found some squares and some semicircles. We all yelled at Poncho for crisscrossing the pie.

"That's it," Poncho said. "From now on everybody chips in the same and we only get an even number of slices."

We sat at the curb underneath the streetlamp and talked baseball. Pizza tasted better in those days.

But it wasn't just the pizza. It may have been an insignificant detail in the record of my youth, as many events are as we mature into adulthood. We learned social interaction, economics, our use of verbal expression, but most of all, the importance of friendship and meaningful relationships.

The Color Test

There is some irony that in a city founded by exiles from intolerance there should occur one of the most disastrous racial riots in the history of the United States. Newark, New Jersey was settled by Robert Treat and his followers in 1666 after a move to escape religious bigotry in New Haven, Connecticut. Three centuries later, amidst the social unrest of the turbulent decade of the 1960s, Newark became the focus of national attention when so many died in the riots and so much property was destroyed.

The Newark that I grew up in the late forties and fifties was just beginning to see expressions of racial unrest, although the racism had been there many years earlier. The Black population had increased dramatically during the so-called Great Migration of 1914 to 1919. African Americans came up from the South in vast numbers to escape a hostile environment of prejudice and poor working conditions exacerbated by the boll weevil affliction of the cotton industry. The Black press aided in spreading the news of good jobs in the industrial North, which faced a manpower shortage since the war had restricted immigration and cut off the source of unskilled European labor. Newark, with its proximity to major industry and the burgeoning New York market, was a prime destination.

While the Black areas of Newark were focused primarily in the districts served by South Side and Central High Schools (later renamed Shabazz and Martin Luther King), East Side, the section where I lived, had a racially diverse population. There were Black enclaves scattered among the Italian, German, Polish, Irish, and Portuguese areas. For the most part, we got along well together, yet respecting one another's turf. There were no major gang fights between Blacks and Whites that I can remember, although other sections of the city could not say as much.

Prejudice is an acquired characteristic. It is not ingrained in one's genes or part of the human racial memory. We are taught fear, hatred, and mistrust by our culture and by our family. Grandmother Wertz was not a racist by any means, although she did use the term "Schwarze" in less-than-approving terms. As a German-speaking immigrant from Russia in the early twentieth century, she was, however, misinformed and could not quite understand American culture. An excellent and creative seamstress, she often made my Halloween costumes. When I was eight years old, she got the idea from a magazine picture for a ghost costume. She made me a costume of a white robe and pointed white hat and white mask. I walked in the Halloween parade not knowing that I was wearing the uniform of the Ku Klux Klan, or not understanding some of the remarks being cast my way. I doubt that Grandmother Wertz even knew what she was setting me up for.

My father was not a racist, although racism was there in subtle ways. The guys that would hang out at my Uncle Pepper's store were sometimes brutal. They had a name for every ethnic group, except perhaps Latvians, most likely because they didn't know anyone of that descent. Blacks, of course, were singled out for the most vicious terms of derision. The Italians, who were also the object of many racial epithets, referred to the Blacks as "Shines," because so many of the boys and men came by with their shoe-shine boxes. My father knew that I had several Black playmates when I was a child and never said anything disparaging about them in particular.

However, that could not be said for one of the regulars at the Broken Hearts Social Club on Elm Street. The club was next to a contractor's business. The yard, where the owner kept an assortment of building materials, was our playground. We shouldn't have been there, but it was fun to play among the material that could be fashioned into hideouts and secret passageways. Snake Eyes Joe came out of the club and caught me and my African American friend Tommy in the yard. Snake Eyes knew my family, so he just gave me a warning, but my Black friend was something else. He placed a brick in my little hands and told me to throw it at him. Instead, I threw at Snake Eyes' legs and Tommy and I both ran from the yard.

Snake Eye's pedagogical techniques were questionable. It was a test, to be sure. He knew that I wouldn't throw the brick. Somehow, I knew that he wouldn't let me. Would Solomon have allowed the infant to be divided between the two women? Would Snake Eyes have been able to stay my hand had I decided to cast the brick? It was not only a test of my ability to harm another human being, but it was also a test of how I perceived the grown-ups in my life. What if I had misunderstood the nature of the lesson and took him at his word?

Throughout my school years, some of the Black kids were my good friends and classmates. There was the scholarly Gene Wiley, intelligent and bright. We had some great conversations together, but later in high school he became aware that his Blackness marked him as decidedly different and would no longer have much to do with his erstwhile White friend. Alfred Wooten was kind and gentle and soft-spoken and later became an ardent follower of Malcolm X. I have wondered if he remained gentle and soft-spoken.

Terry Smith was a wiry kid with the darkest complexion I had ever seen. I inherited his paper route. One time he was showing me the delivery route and we were in a very dark corridor of one of the tenements. I couldn't see him at all. "Terry, where the hell are you? Don't leave me here." Terry smiled and then I saw him—or I should say, I saw his white teeth in the darkness. From then on I called him Cheshire Cat.

Terry's family was among the poorest in the city. They lived in a two-story clapboard house alongside the Jackson Street Bridge. There was no grass in the yard, just dirt and debris and his sisters and brothers. Occasionally a rat would run out from under the house and he would throw a rock at it. He told me that his baby sister had recently been bitten by one. Terry was always dirty and full of scabs. While we played baseball at Riverbank Park on occasion, he was not welcome in our home—not because of the pigment of his skin as much as the dirt on it.

I probably learned more about racism from Dorsey Wilkins than anyone else in Newark. Dorsey was tall, muscular, and confident. He and I worked for Charlie Armel loading ice cream trucks. Dorsey was a Black Muslim and member of the Fruit of Islam, he said. The Fruit of Islam was a kind of security force, an elite group of young Black men who took special vows of virtue and obedience. They were a sort of janissary contingent dedicated to the protection of their leaders.

Dorsey, with his deliberate manner and hard talk against all Whites, inspired a certain fear of the Black movement. This is exactly what he wanted to cultivate. For too long, since the days of slavery, Blacks had lived in fear of the White man. Now the tables were turning and it was the Black man who would instill fear.

He was a fearsome person with his shaven head and swift and purposeful movements. But he spent time with me, not only because I was working with him, but because I was going to college and had a bit more education than the "White trash," as he called them, that made up most of the workforce. He explained the philosophy of the Fruit of Islam—to keep oneself physically, morally, and spiritually fit and to take pride in the Black culture and believe in its eventual world dominance.

There were constant fights between Dorsey and Hank, a battle-wounded veteran of Korea who worked in the freezer. Those who worked in the freezer spent fifteen minutes inside the minus-thirty-degree box and fifteen minutes out. I worked that job one day and can understand how so many had to quit eventually because of crippling arthritis. Those fifteen minutes outside the freezer, however, were the times for the most repartee between the freezer workers and the dock workers. When Dorsey got his hand caught in the freezer door, Hank's remark about taking a bite out of the Fruit of Islam didn't sit too well and Dorsey and he almost came to blows. Most of the time, however, the give-and-take was good-natured and non-volatile.

Martin Luther King Jr. spoke at Franklin and Marshall College across the street from Lancaster Seminary in December 1963. I had a very brief conversation with one of his associates and told him of my intention to join the fight for civil rights. He simply said, "The work is only beginning; there is much to do."

Dorsey helped me understand the reasoning behind the Black culture's feelings and instilled in me a desire to work for racial equality. In my second year in seminary I worked with a group that was organizing participation in the march on Selma. Unfortunately, I ended up in the hospital just before the buses were to leave for Alabama and I missed that historic event.

It is a slow process and there have been setbacks as well as advances. In 1970, when we made our first visit to Wilmington, North Carolina and left the interstate for the final stretch on US 421, I looked out across the darkening fields of tobacco and saw a billboard calling for membership in the United Klans of America. A few years later the sign was gone.

But other signs are still there. If racism is to be eliminated, it needs to be done in every home in America, where attitudes are formed, unkind words spoken, and hatred instilled. Children emulate what they see and hear. Only where there is love and acceptance can there be racial harmony.

Knuckles

Every boy should have a dog. If I had lived on a farm, I would have had Lassie. If I had lived in a New York apartment, I might have had a small terrier. But this was Newark and my father had made his living in the ring, so I got a boxer.

The day my father brought the dog up to our third-floor apartment, the first thing my mother said was, "Harry, you're crazy. This dog's too big. Who's going to take care of it?"

She knew who was going to take care of it. My father had a habit of dropping off strays—dogs and people—for my mother to take care of, and to patch up after fights. This dog was huge. I asked if he had a saddle.

Dad said, "Take him for a walk while I talk with your mother." He handed me the leash; the dog was so excited he jumped up at me and knocked me over and started licking my face. My first thought was, "He's tasting me before he takes a bite." I screamed. Dad got him off me and explained how friendly he was. We headed out the door, an excited dog and a terrified boy. The dog weighed more than I did, and as I stood at the top of the steps I had the thought that he would pull me down both flights. I could hardly control him. I let him go and said, "I'll meet you at the front door."

My plan was to walk him up to the corner and back, but the dog took me for a longer walk. I soon learned that the only way I could restrain him was to wrap his leash around each tree we passed. When I finally got him turned around so that he retraced his steps, he repissed every tree he had marked on the way. It was a chore to get him back up the steps to the apartment.

It was settled; we now had a dog. There was no doubt about it; this was my father's dog, not mine. I was just his caretaker. My father had named the boxer Knuckles for obvious reasons, befitting his and the dog's tough-guy image.

I hated that dog. He was big and ugly. Although not mean, he was demanding. My father would bring his friends around and show off his dog. It wasn't long before I started to become resentful.

And then I got this brilliant idea. I took a small piece of soap, stirred it into Knuckle's food to flavor it, and then slipped it into his water dish. The dog drank the water and the soap and soon began foaming at the mouth. My father and his cronies were watching the Friday night fights in the living room when the dog paid them a visit. One would think that Cerberus had come up from hell the way these grown men scurried in every direction to get out of the apartment. The dog became confused and excited and chased one guy down the steps. Tripping over his own feet, he just managed to slam the screen door when Knuckles smashed into it, putting a larger tear in the existing hole.

It was a hot Friday evening and, as was common, many of the residents and neighbors were sitting on the front steps. This was the primary location for neighborhood socializing and the exchange of gossip. Ralph, who lived on the first floor, had just commented to his wife, Millie, about how quiet it was. There were only two houses on this block of Monroe Street, and the two huge factories at the intersection further reduced the evening traffic. The neighbors were appreciating the momentary lull in the normally busy sounds of the city when the sudden crash of the young man tumbling through the door and down the porch steps caused all heads to turn. What they saw was a big, rabid boxer head protruding through the screen. A mad scramble emptied the steps in an instant as the porch-sitters fled in all directions.

Someone was going next door to call the Humane Society when my mother came down to explain what had happened. I thought I was really in for it, but everyone had a good laugh and the story was retold for years.

Knuckles did not stay long in our apartment. He went on to bigger and better things. Dad arranged for him to do a dog food commercial on television. I thought we were on our way to fame and fortune, but all we got out of that was five cases of dog food. Nevertheless, it was good to have a celebrity in the family. But just when I was starting to like the dog, my father sold him. He was replaced by a miniature boxer, which my mother named Bobo. One day I opened the door and Bobo took off. We never saw him again.

Pets teach us responsibility, care, and love. In later years we did not have dogs, but cats. We don't have to walk cats. Nevertheless, I have learned that there is an element of truth in the saying, "Dogs have masters; cats have staff."

Ghosts of Christmases Past

Most people have their Christmas traditions, whether it is a specific way of decorating the house, or social gatherings, or the placement of a meaningful ornament on the tree. One of my several Christmas traditions is to watch the 1951 version of *A Christmas Carol* with Alastair Sim as Scrooge, considered the finest interpretation of Charles Dickens's classic. I would watch it in the early hours of Christmas morning, and each year apply new interpretations to the story. I saw the contrast between Scrooge's isolation and loneliness and his nephew Fred's desire to include him in his social gathering with Bob Cratchit's close-knit family. When Tiny Tim says, "God bless us—everyone," it includes even Mr. Scrooge. The story had meaning for me on many levels, but most of all, it was about what God has placed in the human heart for all of us to rediscover.

Dickens must have given considerable thought to the naming of Ebenezer Scrooge. "Ebenezer" comes from the Hebrew *'Eben hà-ezer*, meaning "stone of help," and was raised by the prophet Samuel as a memorial of a Hebrew victory over the Philistines. It also serves as a reminder that we too can defeat the dark shadows of our past and be raised victorious to a new life with the help of God, or the presence of God in other people. The eponymous name of Scrooge derives from a Victorian term meaning "squeeze," as both Marley and Scrooge in miserly fashion exacted every cent they could to prosper their business.

Ebenezer Scrooge never really hated Christmas, but rather saw it as an inconvenience. He called it "humbug," or a fraud, a means to either elicit charity or to refrain from productive and material pursuits. One might compare it to modern times when the December mail is saturated with pleas for giving to many worthy causes. "Humbug" might also refer to the over-commercialization of Christmas as the season for spending and buying out of a sense of obligation rather than a desire to express gratitude, appreciation, and love to family and friends. Scrooge may have been right when he saw Christmas as humbug when we forget its real and true meaning. He had to be reminded of its significance by his spectral visitors.

Many of us have our Old Fezziwig memories of good times at Christmastide and see the ghosts of Christmases past in terms of joy, happiness, and love. But, unfortunately, Christmas for many is a sad time when they remember what they have lost. It can be a depressing time of sadness and pain as they see the joy in others that is missing in their own lives.

As a pastor I have had to deal with the tragedy of Christmas in the lives of some of my members. When I was the pastor of the church in Womelsdorf, I would take Communion to Mary. With many shut-in members who live alone, there is a liturgy that precedes the liturgy of the bread and wine, but it is still Communion. It is the liturgy of listening. And so often the stories that I heard were the same stories retold as though for the first time; stories of events that had made such an impact upon the lives of the persons that they had to continually relate the incident over and over again to whomever would listen.

Mary would tell the story of her father's death. She was a teenager at the time, and her father had a long, lingering illness. It was Christmas Eve and she was to join the youth from the church in Christmas caroling, but her father's condition had deteriorated. No sooner had he drawn his last breath and passed away than Mary heard the carolers outside her window. They were singing "Joy to the World."

The incongruity and irony had never been forgotten, and for more than fifty years Mary would retell that story. In the midst of her grief she heard a song of joy. It may not have been the message she wanted to hear, but she needed the tidings of comfort. The memory of the passing of a loved one at Christmas can endure for years and forever cast its shadow on how the holiday is observed.

It was a Christmas Eve morning when the phone rang. I was preparing for the joyous celebration of God's presence when I had to face the terrible blackness of God's absence. They found the body of our church's youth worker behind the wheel of his car. The long-barreled gun between his legs had shattered how we would celebrate Christ's birth that evening. Chris had his reasons. He lived in his own darkness and despair, a torment of the soul that engulfed him like the blackness of a great abyss and brought him to his doom. We often do not know what occurs in the minds and lives of people we know, even those close to us, but we trust that the issues that they face will have resolution on the other side of this life when they cannot find fulfillment in this phase of existence. The meaning of Christmas is that God surrounds us with love and life, now and forever.

Facing one's own death is hard for many people, but sometimes comfort and assurance comes from the other side of life. One Christmas Eve I visited Katie, who was terminally ill with cancer. Her daughter had moved her bed downstairs to the dining room, which was more accessible for caregivers and visitors. Katie told me that she had awakened from a dream in the early hours of that morning and looked up from her bed to see her brother standing in the doorway to the kitchen. Her brother had died several years earlier and he had not been in her recent memory. He had simply smiled and said to her, "I will see you soon," and was gone. Katie died the evening of the next day—Christmas Day.

Ruth was one of our shut-in members. A devoted member of the church, she was in her nineties and lived alone. When I visited with her during Christmas week, I noticed piles and piles of Christmas cards, some posted around doorways, opened on shelves, or just lying on the coffee table. I remarked at how many she had received. She said that they were all old cards; she received none from the current year. "I bring out the old cards to remember family and friends who are gone." And then a question I wasn't prepared for: "Why do we have to die?" Before I could answer, she said, "I can't wait to join them."

John overdosed at a Christmas party while the rest of his family were in church for the candlelight Christmas Eve service. He pulled through, but after the service his brother and I went to visit him at the hospital. "Better living through chemistry" is not always the case, and how drugs can enhance a time of conviviality and *joie de vivre* is most questionable. For many, heroin is not for pleasure but for escape, and at Christmastime a means of avoiding painful memories that are exacerbated when others are enjoying life and you are not.

Scrooge's ghostly visitors remind him that he has lost his connectedness to others and is lacking in relationships that make us human. Christmas Past conjures memories of happier days when Scrooge enjoyed the company of others and of the love he lost when he followed after material things. Christmas Present presents him with the opportunity of helping his employee Bob Cratchit and the crippled Tiny Tim, as well as reconnecting with his nephew. Christmas Yet to Come confronts Scrooge with his death as separation from the life of relationships with others and the meaninglessness of the pursuit of happiness in materialism.

Christmas reminds us that we are all related in the mind of God. Friends and family are important. When we witness the loss of lives in our culture from homicides, mass killings, COVID deaths, and other disasters, we realize how necessary and important we are to each other.

My ghosts come to me each year, not only to remind me of happy times, but to assure me that God is always present. God is the fount of all our blessings, and at Christmas we raise our Ebenezers as a reminder that we are never really alone. We just need to be aware of the light that comes from Bethlehem's manger to assure us that God is with us in those who love us.

The Other Side of the Mirror

———

Alice entered her wonderland of fantasy and illusion by escaping through the looking glass that mirrored her world, and was able to experience another reality that was just as real to her as the one she escaped.

My mirror of escape was the Metropolitan Museum of Art in New York. My first visit was when I was eleven years old. It was only a forty-cent bus ride from Penn Station in Newark to Port Authority in New York, and then a long walk up Eighth Avenue, past the frontiers of civilization, the porn shops, gin joints, decayed buildings, and scary-looking people. And then Columbus Circle and its gateway to Central Park, which was much more inviting and less foreboding than it has become. I would eventually make my way to Fifth Avenue and East Eighty-Fourth, where Uncle Emilio lived and had his art studio. I didn't visit Emilio much in those days, but it was a comfort to know that he was close by if needed.

Entering the Met was like climbing Mount Olympus or entering the halls of Valhalla. Here were all the treasures of human civilization, the vast riches of art and beauty assembled and arrayed before me, and for a few hours they were all mine as I went from room to room in my great palace. Uniformed servants stood at the entrance to every room, eager to respond to any question I might have. I could linger before cases of jeweled croziers and reliquaries, gaze at towering portraits of centuries-old *illuminati*, and walk among the marble heads of Roman emperors.

Here were magnificent paintings and sculptures depicting the myths and legends of Greece and Rome, many of the stories my father had taught me, and many new ones that would send me back to the library for further explanation. Here was the undraped female form laying bare the mysteries that a young boy could only wonder at, and wondering what distorted vision a Rubens or a Duchamps could have. Here were the halls of death of ancient Egypt and the observation that it was only because of their preoccupation with the afterlife that they preserved so many artifacts in this life. Here also was an amazing display of medieval arms and armor, the cutting edges of a feudal world of rank and privilege, where combat became entertainment, not unlike the early twenty-first century. All sorts of ingenious devices for inflicting torture and death were showcased. Horses and dogs, covered in metal plate, also had their place in this warrior world.

I never noticed how much art and beauty were connected with death and destruction. The grave monuments from the ancient world, the Renaissance tombs, the exquisite designs engraved into swords and firearms, paintings of armies in combat and distinguished historical figures in military dress—all glorify war and attempt to ennoble the ancient art of killing.

Unlike a photograph, the artist selects that which he or she will preserve, and determines the context in which the work is seen. A photograph is less discriminating, and while a photographer can direct the lens and compose the subject, the film or digital image sensor records whatever is before it. A photographic portrait offers less mercy than a canvas, or as some of my Pennsylvania Dutch friends would say to those who complain about their picture, "What looks in, looks out." I began to see as the artist saw, how what he incorporated into his painting was often dictated by his culture and what he was conditioned by his environment to see. We do not examine the lens by which we view our world, but merely place our faith in its accuracy and accept that what we see is what is. The beauty and wonder of observing art is that what the artist intends is only part of the process of interpretation. What I was seeing was also based upon what I was conditioned to see. Anais Nin was so right: "We see the world not as it is, but as we are."

When I first saw the painting of Joan of Arc by Jules Bastien-Lepage, I was fascinated by the mystery of the archangel's appearance, how Michael was there and not there. It was like seeing another world superimposed on my own. This contrasted with the young Joan, a girl of pure innocence accepting a challenge greater than her position in life, stubborn because she knew she had powerful friends in high places.

Years later, the picture has lost some of its transcendent qualities. It no longer presents an illusory world, and Joan seems more of a peasant girl with a bewildered look. The painting, of course, hasn't changed at all, but I have, and how I look at it.

In Oscar Wilde's novel *The Picture of Dorian Gray*, the portrait takes on all the attributes of Gray's dissolute life. Dorian Gray's wish is that he would remain forever young and handsome while his picture would take on the effects of his debauchery. One interpretation is that it is not the portrait that changes, but Dorian Gray's perception of himself. In the end he does not look at a fixed portrait, but at a mirror of himself that horrifies him and destroys him. I believe that all that we do in life is accumulated in a portrait that is presented to us at the last judgment for our own review and critique.

In another portrait story, Robert Nathan's *Portrait of Jennie*, an imaginary girl comes into the life of an artist at certain points in his life to remind him of love, innocence, purity, and she remains forever young because she represents those qualities that are eternal.

Alice Neel was a painter who said about her subjects that they assumed a pose that demonstrated "what the world has done to them . . ." We become caricatures of what we envision ourselves to be, or what the world has forced us to become in spite of our vision.

In the second half of my life, I return to the Metropolitan Museum of Art and visit all the "still unravished brides of quietness" which continue to evoke all the awe and wonder that they had years ago, but in delightful new ways. In the same way, I can return again and again to the words of Scripture to discover what new light God is breaking forth. Our lives change; our needs change; our learning increases; our perspective is altered by the events of our times. Because we are different, our mirrored images change, but on the other side of the mirror is God's unalterable truth, which we shall all confront in the final day.

Memorial Fruitcake

My mother saved virtually everything. When she passed away after living into her nineties, my brother and I had the responsibility of cleaning out her house. It was a formidable job of sifting through financial records dating back more than fifty years, books she had ordered and probably never got around to reading, dishes and kitchenware tucked into every nook and cranny. Her many friends over the years would give her gifts of expensive wine and liquor that accumulated on the dining room floor unopened.

Since Tillie had spent her last years at my brother's home, the detritus of her living just sat there in her small home on Marne Street in the Ironbound section of Newark. Our biggest fear was opening her refrigerator and being exposed to the biohazard within. We strapped it closed and had it hauled away without even checking its contents.

It reminded me of another woman who was cleaning out her mother's freezer and discovered a turkey that had been there for twenty-five years. She decided to call a nearby university's home economics department to ask if the turkey was safe to eat. After being told that it might be dangerous and make her very sick, she said, "That's what I thought. I don't want it to go to waste, so I guess I will just give it to our local food bank."

There should be some limits to our generosity.

My Aunt Anna was the quintessential cook. Her culinary presentations were out of this world. She was so good that her grandson learned from her, went on to study at the Culinary Institute in New York, and now conducts cooking tours of Italy and teaches in Tuscany. Aunt Anna's *pièce de résistance* was her fruitcake, to which everyone looked forward at Christmas dinner. Before she died, she gave the recipe to her sister. Aunt

Mary is what my German grandmother would call *doppich*, a word that is also in the Pennsylvania German dialect. The kitchen was *terra incognita*. When Anna would ask her to boil water, Mary would ask for how long, and you would never ask her for an omelet unless you enjoy eggshells.

Nevertheless, the year after Anna died, Mary attempted the fruit cake. Not only was it the worst fruit cake that was ever made, but to add insult to indigestion, she made two of them. No one would cut into that second fruitcake, and so it became the gag gift of the Serio clan. Each year an unsuspecting soul would receive it for Christmas. And it made its rounds year after, long after Mary's death. Each time we would remember with nostalgic longing the sheer delight of Anna's table, and with kindly affection and much laughter, Mary's good-hearted attempt to succeed her sister.

But nothing is forever—neither turkeys, nor fruit cakes, nor good times and bad, nor loved ones who gave us so much joy. Year after year, we lose a little more time and build a generous supply of memories.

June Sprigg is the author of almost two dozen books about the Shakers, a nearly extinct species of American religion. June grew up in Martins Creek, where I spent the first four years of my ministry. I would see her from time to time, usually at funerals or weddings, and I always asked her how she liked life among the Shakers. In her book *Simple Gifts*, she details the summer she spent living in Canterbury Village, New Hampshire among the last surviving Shakers. We know the Shakers as creators of very simple and functional furniture, but their spiritual life was also simple and functional. They simply took delight in the presence of God and saw God's activity in their daily lives, in the persons who lived in their community, and in those who visited.

I have come to appreciate those spiritual expressions that follow Brother Lawrence's simplicity of "practicing the presence of God" and the Westminster Catechism which says "man's chief end is to glorify God and enjoy him forever."

Celtic spirituality also expresses gratitude for God's presence and recognizes the spirit of God in every moment of life and in every situation in which one finds oneself. The early prayers of the Celtic church always asked for God's help and deliverance in times of danger, particularly from the fury of the Northmen, whose constant raids ravished their settlements. When all else fails, only God is left. Therefore, in an uncertain and dangerous world one learns the principle of *carpe diem*, of seizing the present moment and being grateful for what you have *now*. Then you can piece together all of these now moments for a life of eternal thanksgiving.

Each year we celebrate the holiday in a *time of plenty*. We have an abundance of almost everything. Our grain fields continue to produce sufficiently to meet our needs. The unemployment rate in 2022 was at its lowest point ever. We can also be grateful that the nation has endured and preserved the blessings of God, sometimes because of our leaders and sometimes in spite of them.

But we are also mindful that we live in the midst of tragedy. Our hearts continue to be wounded by acts of violence and terrorism, and we seem confused by Jesus' words to feed the hungry and welcome the stranger at our gates. We have somehow lost the biblical sense of hospitality, and God's commandment to give shelter and protection to refugees, even at our own risk. Our ancestors were once strangers in a strange land who were given food and shelter by Native Americans.

We ought to remember that Thanksgiving is in reality a religious holiday. There is a danger in making our country a substitute for God. That's not what the Pilgrim fathers wanted. After all, they had fled to these shores not really for democratic freedom but because of religious persecution in Europe. They wanted the right to worship God as they saw fit. That first Thanksgiving was a testimony of God's goodness in spite of all that had befallen the colonists during their first winter of death and despair.

It is possible that those early pilgrims might have had something resembling a fruitcake. They had fruits and they made cakes out of the grain they had. It is said that those early New Englanders would place five grains of corn at their plates so as not to forget the hardship that the first settlers endured. And yet, in spite of the harshness of the winter, the hunger, and the sickness and death of so many, it was only the sailors that returned to England aboard the Mayflower.

We should not forget that story. It's part of the heritage of the United Church of Christ, since members of that denomination are the spiritual descendants of the Pilgrims and the Puritans, as well as the Pennsylvania German farmers.

Several years ago I performed a baptism for one of our church members who traces her ancestry back to the Mayflower, and is a descendant of its builder, John Vassail. As we shared her story, we remembered that her ancestors came here as refugees to seek a new and better life, to escape the wars and persecution they suffered because of religious fanaticism. Because they endured, we have prospered.

When my family would gather for the traditional Thanksgiving meal, the table was laden with a huge variety of food, many of the dishes representing the Old World countries that my family came from. Anna's fruitcake would be brought out, not to be consumed, but to be passed on to the next custodian.

I don't remember the last steward of the fruitcake, but it was getting to be quite old. I think Uncle John suggested donating it to the food kitchen that served the homeless on Mulberry Street.

War Stories

I officiated at the funeral for my Aunt Dotty. Her funeral was held before the obituary appeared in the paper, so there were very few at her service. Nevertheless, it was a time for memory and family reflections. It took an hour and a half to drive to the cemetery, a veterans' cemetery that is near McGuire Air Force Base, where she was to be buried next to her husband. During that drive, I had the time to reflect on their lives, especially Frank, who was a sergeant with the Army Rangers during the Second World War. He saw action at Guadalcanal, the Philippines, and other famous as well as some obscure places. The stories he told were rich with action and adventure, hardship and humor. When the family would gather for Sunday supper, we would watch the television series *Victory at Sea*, and Frank would provide his own running commentary and inside information that embellished the narrative. But when he would talk about the buddies he lost and the enemies that were killed, he would sometimes choke with emotion. Like many experiences, one may be able to share the facts of the story, but another can never know the experience as one who had lived through it. Even as the memory of those experiences helped to shape his life and the values that he would instill in his family, so too those shared experiences would affect me and the views that I have formulated over the years.

There is a movie that was overlooked by many. It is the story of Antwone Fisher. It is a true story of a boy whose father had been killed before he was born and whose mother gave birth to him inside the Ohio State Prison. He was raised in a foster home that was abusive on many levels, but eventually he ran away and joined the Navy. His volatile temper and latent anger put him in contact with the base psychologist, who suggested that he go back to find the family he lost and to confront the mother who had abandoned him. It is a story of memory and healing, because how we remember our past makes us who we are. Often, before we can deal with our future, we must be able to deal with our past and bring reconciliation and wholeness to the relationships that were once fragmented. Sometimes it is a matter of forgiving those who injured us, and sometimes it is seeking pardon from those whom we injured. But having done that, one must move toward the future and leave the past where it is. Like Lot's wife, if we look back to the past with longing for what once was, we become frozen in time, and incapable of forging a new life.

Psalm 98 has a lesson for us. It is a psalm that speaks of memory and of newness, of victory and vindication, of joy and praise. Although the verbs in this psalm are past tense, the reference is to a future event. This is typical of so much of Scripture, where the biblical writers speak not only of past and current events, but describe them in terms of what is yet to be. The writer reaches into the past to make a future prediction.

Thus Jesus can speak of past events as though they are prophetic descriptions of what he is accomplishing. In the same way, the present plants the seeds for the future. Jesus tells the disciples, "If you keep my commandments, you will abide in my love" (John 15:10).

It is interesting that he uses this word "abide" five times in three verses. "Abide" has several definitions and they all seem appropriate. The word can mean to remain in one place, or to live with, as in an "abode." It may also mean to be faithful and steadfast. These definitions have the connotation of being fixed in the present moment. For example, the prophet Malachi (3:2), in the King James Version of the Bible, says, "But who shall abide the day of his coming, and who shall stand when he appeareth." Past, present, and future are all wrapped together, for in the mind of God there is no time. In the bulb there is a flower; from the past will come the future.

But it is precisely in those times of deep despair that we need to sing the Lord's song, the new songs of what God is doing in our lives and what God will continue to do in our lives.

We need to remember the past; we need to confront the past; but we must not abide in the past. As Tom Wingfield says in the opening lines of *The Glass Menagerie*, "The play is memory." Life is memory, and how we remember it will determine what songs we shall sing. Memories change with time. In his final speech, when Tom talks about how it feels to remember his family, he says, "Time is the longest distance between two places." James

Joyce once said that imagination is memory. What we imagine is created not from the past that really happened, but from our imperfect remembrances of the past we wanted, desired, and dreamed about. We construct our own reality from the fragments we select, whether true or not.

On Memorial Day, when we take time to remember those whose sacrifices have made our nation what it is, we also remember all the people whose lives have affected our own. If the memories are painful and you are only selecting fragments, then you need to seek healing. If they are good memories, give thanks to God and build on them. But in any case, move on and sing a new song, for God has done marvelous things and continues to do so.

The movie *Antwone Fisher* ends as it began, with a dream in which young Antwone is led into a barn where African American ancestors, representing every generation from slavery to present day, stand ready to welcome him. He is seated at the head of the table, a place of honor, with a grand feast placed before him. He is nurtured and nourished by his past, even as we become who we are based upon the love and nurture we have received from our families and others.

Uncle Frank told many stories, most of them lost and filed away somewhere. There is one story that I remember clearly. Frank was bivouacked with his platoon in an open field. It was toward the end of the war, but there was still fighting to be done. A group of Japanese soldiers appeared out of the jungle and marched straight through the middle of the resting American troops. The Americans were dumbfounded. They could not fire on the enemy for fear of hitting their own men, and the Japanese soon disappeared into the jungle on the other side of the clearing. It was an unarranged and spontaneous cease-fire.

A friend of my family who fought against the Nazis told of another impromptu truce on Christmas in 1944. Unlike the First World War, where the two armies exchanged food and pleasantries, there were a few isolated incidents where opposing soldiers put down their weapons and recognized that they were all children of the same God.

When I remember the war stories that my Uncle Frank told, and how America was engaged in a devastating war against Germany and Japan, I realize that these erstwhile enemies are now among our closest allies and trading partners. The world continues to change and we must be patient with ourselves and with each other. Let us remember that we are all part of the human family and the world can only get better when we contribute our concern, interest, love, and nurture to creating the realm of God on earth.

Faraway Places
with Strange-Sounding Names

As a young child growing up in northern New Jersey, I was familiar with the nearby communities and the big city across the Hudson River. I would sometimes visit the shore towns and their beaches, but anything west of the Delaware River was a huge wasteland filled with cows and buggies and men with beards, and further west they rode horses and shot each other. I knew the names of some of the places.

Grandmother Natalie would tell me stories of the places where she grew up in imperial Russia: Tsaritsyn, Gorodishche, Saratov. She would remember other places she had visited or stopped at on her voyage to America. Though she was an ethnic German, I would never tell anyone that she and my grandfather were born in Russia, which at the height of the Cold War was then the Soviet Union. During the Second World War, I would listen to the radio and hear about strange places in Europe where American forces were engaged, and after the war, Uncle Frank would tell me of the places in the Pacific where he had fought. I could hardly envision this world of faraway places with strange-sounding names.

Around the corner from our apartment on Monroe Street, there was a large house with a big front window. Mr. Neto would sit at his desk in front of the window with his stamp collection, pasting the little pieces of paper in his large books.

At first, stamp collecting didn't make much sense to me and Mr. Neto seemed a bit too reclusive to approach. However, one day I found an envelope with an unusual stamp on it and a word that I could not pronounce.

When I saw Mr. Neto sitting on his front stoop, I asked about the value of the stamp. He invited me inside and opened up his stamp catalog and showed me that the letters spelled Hellas in Greek. I was hooked. This brief encounter opened the door to a fascinating world of geography, politics, and culture. I would now spend my meager allowance buying stamps from Mr. Neto.

Today, with so many perverts in our society, one would be rather wary about being invited into a home of an elderly single gentleman, but that was a time when fear was a world away. My fear was in holding a German stamp with the face of Adolf Hitler on it.

The Down Neck area of Newark was a hodgepodge of ethnicities, colors, and nationalities, of which I became increasingly aware delivering newspapers to families with unusual names and accents.

This exposure in my childhood to the variety of places and languages left me with a desire to see many of the countries I had heard about. I have visited more than fifty countries, some more than once, and have lived and worked in many places. Although some of my colleagues and missionary associates can claim a much greater travel list, it was sufficient for me to appreciate a world of infinite variety and points of view.

I was in London and staying with the family of Kenneth French, the vicar of Paddington Chapel. At dinner one day, his daughter turned to me and bluntly asked, "Why do you Americans hate the Communists so much?" That caught me off guard, but opened up a dialogue of political and social import, and I assured her that "hate" was too strong a word for some people, especially those of us working within the church.

Outside of Dunfermline Abbey in Scotland, I was talking with a friend when a Scotsman, recognizing my accent, came up to me. He wanted to shake my hand because Americans had rescued him during a battle engagement in Italy. Somehow we were comrades in arms even though I was just a toddler during the war. I wish I had the time to listen to his story, but the brief encounter had its own message. In the midst of war's division, there was a degree of unity.

When the World Ministries Board of the United Church of Christ met in our area, I displayed the flags of all the countries represented by our ministries. Moses Awatona, an exchange student from Kenya at Kutztown University who attended our church, recognized his flag and stood up with great pride and was so happy that it was being displayed. It was another point of union with another part of the world.

When we understand our differences and talk with one another, we learn to appreciate our common humanity and can celebrate that we are at heart children of the one creator God. People's lives may be shaped by where they live, by the languages they use, by so many other factors. It is only when we communicate that we are able to understand one another, for that is the very derivation of the word "communicate"—"to share in common."

Jackson Whites, Gullah Geechees, and Doukhobors

The city of Newark, like many large urban areas, especially Philadelphia, is made up of a variety of neighborhoods, each with its own distinct origin and character. Some neighborhoods were intriguing and inviting, others were foreboding. As a teenager, I wanted to explore and experience the fascinating subcultures of my city.

Mulberry Street was where a farmer's market was set up each week and you could go and buy fresh produce. It was also like New York's Bowery, where the homeless would gather and beg for handouts. There were several social services offering shelter, soup kitchens, employment, and health care. Some of my friends called it "Bum's Street," but that only reflected their insensitivity.

Chinatown was at the other end of Mulberry, across Market Street, and a favorite eating location, but you had to go past several bawdy houses to get there. There were also some reputed opium dens. Coming out of a restaurant on one occasion, I walked past one of these houses of ill repute. At the top of a flight of steps was a very attractive young woman in a silk dress with a long slit up the side. She beckoned to me. I smiled and moved quickly down the street. Temptation can be scary.

The Black section was north of the courthouse, and those from the east side would seldom venture into this area. The great migration of African Americans following the two world wars looking for work in the industrial North settled in this area. Here were some of the city's great jazz clubs. Newark was the birthplace of many jazz greats such as Sarah Vaughn,

Whitney Houston, and Woody Shaw, as well as other great singers and musicians like Paul Simon and Connie Francis.

I lived in the Ironbound section, known as "Down Neck" because it was originally a narrow strip of inhabited dwellings along Ferry Street that led to the ferry to New York. Newark's East Ward was a conglomeration of many smaller neighborhoods, a mix of European ethnicities, each with its own territorial church. One could easily move among Italian, German, Spanish, Portuguese, Russian, Polish, and other settlements. My neighborhood was German with streets originally named for German cities like Hamburg, Bremen, and Berlin, but they were renamed during the First World War and became Wilson, Marne, and Rome.

One summer's day, walking back from the Newark Museum, I paused for a break on a bench in Military Park and observed the passersby. Most were businesspeople, shoppers, and some tourists, but one man in particular was most frightening. An older man sitting on the bench beside me noted my startled reaction and proceeded to describe the man I had just seen. He was one of the Jackson Whites, a group of often albino, polydactyl mountain folk from the Ramapo Mountains near the New Jersey–New York border. They occasionally came to Newark.

The Jackson Whites are a mixed-race enclave of people who lived in relative isolation to the north. During the Revolutionary War, the British hired mercenaries from Hesse in Germany. Some of these Hessian soldiers deserted and found refuge among the Native Americans living in the Ramapo region as well as Dutch White settlers. Many of the Natives were themselves outcasts from various tribes. Joining this group were runaway African slaves and even some prostitutes that the British had brought up from the West Indies to service their troops. This motley group became derogatorily called "Jackson Whites," presumably a corruption of "Jacks and Whites," "Jacks" being a racial slur for Black slaves.

The Jackson Whites are only one of the many subcultures that make America the great melting pot. I have always been fascinated with these groups that have been able to resist the tendency to merge with the mainstream and have maintained their culture, ethnicity, and beliefs in spite of all the forces at work to compel assimilation.

It is sometimes difficult to see the forest because of the trees, so if you live in eastern Pennsylvania, you don't often look around and consider the Pennsylvania Dutch as a subculture, although you might be fascinated by Amish and Mennonite groups who are also in the area. There are hundreds of subcultures within this country, many of them obscure, but with their own intriguing histories, heritage, and stories.

Off the coast of South Carolina and Georgia are the Sea Islands, commonly called the "Gullah" or "Geechee." Here descendants of African slaves still live, speaking a *patois* of West African, Creole, and English languages and preserving a culture far different from most African Americans today. When visiting my brother-in-law in Wilmington, North Carolina, we would sometimes drive down to Cape Fear. Wilmington was the northern extremity of a corridor that stretched to Florida. Along this coastal area was where the Gullah people lived. They are sometimes referred to as "Geechee." Unfortunately, this subculture has been exploited by developers, and their settlements replaced by resorts, opulent estates, and gated communities.

Julie Dash, a writer and producer, spent four years producing the film *Daughters of the Dust*, about one particular family and their struggle to resist assimilation.

The major difference between African and American culture that surfaces in the film is religious and spiritual. Most Americans tend to be dualists in that they separate the spiritual life from the material life. Americans, living in a country two and a half centuries old, still have a frontier mentality of rugged individualism, of going it alone, of disregarding the rest of the human race in order to meet their own agenda. We don't seem to mind being isolated and disconnected. From the fierce singularity of the New England farmer to the Western pioneer seizing land by conquest from the original Native Americans, we have been taught to value individuality.

On the other hand, the structure of traditional African philosophy sees all living things as organically connected, interrelated, and interdependent. Unlike the dominant Western view in which spirit and matter are distinct and irreconcilable, African philosophy and religion are based on a conception of being as an invisible and an unbroken circle of spirits—from conception to birth through life to death. In this view there is a sense of connection, an unbroken line reaching back to creation in which all ancestors are linked to those not yet born. There is no separation between sacred and secular life, but all people are tied together in one bundle of life.

My own maternal ancestry is Volga German, predominantly ethnic German Protestant immigrants from Russia who settled mostly in middle America. My mother's parents emigrated from the Saratov and Tsaritsyn area and took up residence in a German enclave in Newark, and became members of an evangelical German church where worship was in the

German language. America, being the great assimilator of nations, also welcomed other subcultures from Russia and the rest of the world. I took an interest in the Doukhobors, who settled mainly in Canada, with some in the northern United States. They were an early "spiritual but not religious" group, who eschewed Russian Orthodox rituals and practices and sought extra-biblical revelation. Having endured much turmoil and persecution in Russia, they became pacifists who focused on the indwelling spirit of God. They secured a great deal of support from the Quakers and Leo Tolstoy, who donated the profits from one of his books to help them emigrate to North America.

There is an amazingly large list of ethnic subcultures in the United States, such as Native Americans, varieties of Latin Americans, Asian Americans and so on, as well as more obscure groups like the Irish Travelers and Romani.

Mary Ann and I were staying with some of her relatives in Budapest, Hungary and she expressed a desire to visit a gypsy camp. I suppose we had a romantic view of fun-loving gypsy rovers—exotic violins playing in presto tempo, wild dancing, and a carefree living out of horse-drawn wagons. Josef, her cousin, expressed shock at her request, but wanting to be an accommodating host, he took us to the gypsy neighborhood. It was not what we expected. Josef explained that gypsies didn't belong in his country, although they were Hungary's largest minority at a half-million people. They were called "Roma" and had their origins on the Indian subcontinent, but traveled throughout Europe working at menial jobs and begging, and were known to engage in petty thievery. They were citizens of Hungary, living in the country, but not part of the tradition and culture. They were resident aliens, often feared by Hungarians. Our trip through the camp was rather rapid, since Josef refused to stop, believing that we might be accosted.

The world is not a neat and orderly place with people of a certain ethnic identity remaining within the confines of their own country. When the world is in turmoil, people move. Rwandans take refuge in Uganda; Iraqis escape to Syria; Afghans flee the Taliban; Greeks move to Germany; Central Americans move to the United States looking for jobs and a better life. Ukrainians seek refuge in Europe to escape the Russian onslaught. The United Nations High Commissioner for Refugees has over twenty-one million people under his mandate, people looking to escape war and destruction in their native lands.

With so many subcultures, indigenous peoples, and immigrants being absorbed into the American stew and being rejected by radical pseudo-patriots, we are losing so much of what has made the United States a shining beacon for the world. Liberty's lamp beside the golden door is slowly being quenched in the waters of ignorance, intolerance, and bigotry.

As the Advent hymn suggests, we live in lonely exile here, waiting for the Son of God to appear.[1] We must come to the realization that God is among us and that we are no longer aliens, no longer strangers in a strange land, no longer wanderers in a hostile universe. Our true comfort is in knowing that we belong, body and soul, to a loving God who cares for all of God's children, and that in the end we shall realize that we are one people.

---

1. "O Come, O Come, Emmanuel," words translated by J. M. Neale (1851).

Down by the Old Mill Stream

There are places in our lives that hold special meaning and significance, places to which we want to return, whether physically or in memory. They are places that shape our lives, foster and develop meaningful relationships, determine our future, and guide us in exploring the spiritual dimension of our being. For many persons it may be a geographical location, or a place in time, or an association with other persons such as peers, family, teachers, spiritual leaders, or friends. Very often it comprises all of these.

For me it was the church camp at Mensch Mill, located in a then very rural section of Berks County, Pennsylvania, some hundred miles distant from my home in the New Jersey–New York cosmopolis.[1] Early on, in 1925, the Evangelical and Reformed Church, now the United Church of Christ, began the search for a place where young people might gather for conferences that would enhance their spiritual growth. One of the leaders of this committee was the Rev. Dr. Fred Wentzel, who at the time was a predecessor of mine at Christ UCC, in Temple, Pennsylvania. I often think of how synchronistic it was that for all the churches I served in my conference, their previous pastors were all leaders in the camping movement.

Adam L. Mensch operated grist, cider, and saw mills on the bank of a stream fed by the waters of the Perkiomen Creek, Northwestern Branch. The first mill built by White settlers dated back to 1733, the ruins of which were still there when the site was purchased. Historically, this had always

---

1. The Rev. William H. Solly was Minister of Camping for many years. I had worked closely with him as secretary of the East Penn Camps executive committee. Bill prepared an exhaustive record of the story of the church camps in an unpublished manuscript entitled "The Evolution of Mensch Mill and the Fernbrooks."

been a mill site, for the Lenni Lenape peoples would grind their grain into flour in a place where the narrow stream enters the pond. Mr. Mensch said that he had one of the pestles in his office. The existing mill was built in 1822. Over the years, additional acreage and buildings were added to the church camp, in particular the Jacob Rupp farm, with farmhouse and barn.

The eighty-two-year-old miller sold his property in 1929 for six thousand dollars to the church, reducing his original price by five hundred dollars because it was the church. It consisted of forty-three acres, on which were located the mill, house, barn, piggery, a mill pond which would be used for swimming and boating, and other smaller buildings.

Many years ago, a camper by the name of Gilbert J. Bartholomew wrote a pamphlet entitled "Reflections," about a place that is sacred to the memory of hundreds of people.

> An old camper was returning to the place that was most dear to his heart, most sacred to his memory, most beautiful in his life. To the melody of the birds' song and rhythm of the rippling stream, he came winding his way over the lower road, arched by an arbor of softly-swaying boughs and trembling leaves of oak, elm, and maple. He was approaching silently, humbly, reverently, for the ground whereon he was treading was Holy Ground.

Gil may have been referring to his "morning watch" location at Mensch Mill, but I have never failed to think of our camps as "holy ground," sanctified by our communion not only with God, but also with the earth and with one another.

In this period of history, when climate change is eroding our planet, the environmentalists are reminding us that our "mother is dying" and that radical changes are needed. We need to redefine a theology of the earth, of understanding our relationship with our planet and the rest of the created order. When one learns to think in terms of the Gaia principle, that earth is an organic whole in which all creatures are part of its life force which determines its destiny, we gain a new concept of what it means to be stewards of creation. We were not put in the garden to exploit it, but to care for it. When God directed Adam, the operative word was *shamar*—to keep, to preserve, to maintain the life of the earth. We are God's representative on the earth and charged to love and serve the world, to love nature as God the creator loves the object of her creation.

Every year when I would come to Camp Mensch Mill and leave behind the urban wilderness of macadam, steel, and brick, and feel the soft earth beneath my feet, I knew that I was in a special place. It is special because it is itself a symbol of God's presence. We need to become panentheists—people who discern the presence of God in the created order. We need to think of what the church has called "outdoor ministry" not only as a ministry that is conducted *in* the out-of-doors, but as a ministry *to* the out-of-doors, a ministry to the earth. Church camping immediately sets apart the camper from everyday routine. The camper knows upon arrival that something special is going to occur in this place. While holy ground is always under one's feet, it is in this place that one is prepared for the encounter, and expectant of it.

A young camper does not come to camp to meet God. He or she comes to have a good time, to be with other people. That sense of fellowship is vital to any experience. One of the greatest feelings of solitude is to be that last camper to leave at the end of an event. When the sounds of play and laughter and singing have gone, you realize how important other people are to your own development and maturity. Young people have used the camping experience as a testing ground for behavior and thinking, because they know that it is of limited duration and that they don't have to live forever with their social *faux pas*. They also know that when a sense of community has developed, they will have the affirmation of their fellow campers and the guidance of their counselors to help them in their social adjustment. The camping experience, because it is short-lived, provides a balance to the sustained relationships of the church and school environments.

There is a sense of history and heritage associated with the camps. One realizes that he or she is a part of a tradition, of a fellowship that extends beyond the immediate. This helps create a linkage, a kind of bonding to the larger fellowship of the church, not only in space, but also in time. The camping experience becomes a kind of repository for those indefinable feelings and memories that are never written down, but are transmitted from one generation to the next, like the words to a song that every camper knows but can't find in any songbook. There are many of us who have come to realize and appreciate that one of the deepest roots in our lives is the one that has tapped the underground spring of church camping, and found that we have continued to absorb its nurturing waters.

If I am asked for a sign of God's presence at our camp, I would say that it is not only the natural beauty of the environment, but the love that is shared in community, in the sound of singing and laughter, in the sight of a campfire's glow beneath a starry sky, and in the ground itself. God is always present in fellowship and shared love, and in the silence of the woods where one speaks to God. It is in the silence that one hears the other voices of God's creatures, the *anawim*, the poor and lowly who depend upon God, and whose cries are often lost when we are too busy doing other things.

We cannot ever cut ourselves off from this relationship to our camping tradition. Holy ground is sanctified by our encounter with God and by God's activity in human activity, which expresses God's love to the created order. We need to reaffirm a theology of place, but a place where one is in communion with others, and a bond of love and friendship is created and endures.

During the summer camping program, there were many opportunities for prayer and worship. For many campers it was in the words and the singing of camp songs, whether after meals in the dining hall, or on a hike, or on the porch of Pilgert's store in the village of Huffs Church. Music brought us together. However, there were other special places and times when the presence of the Holy was most definitely experienced.

Every evening, as the sun was setting, we would make the trek up to Vesper Hill for a moment of prayer. As one entered the canopy of pine trees leading to the summit, absolute silence was maintained so that one could hear the many voices of the earth and its creatures. The view from the hill of the distant landscape in the fading light spoke more than words could, and between the words spoken by worship leaders one heard the sound of God in the silence.

In the evening of the night before the closing of the camp, a bonfire was set in the council circle. Again, we made our way through the woods in silence, and at the conclusion of the worship we lit our candles, passing the flame from one to another, and then made our way back to the pond. More than a hundred lights circled the lake as we sang taps, extinguished the flames, and made our quiet way back to the cabins. The only sounds were the occasional tears of some of the campers whose lives had been profoundly changed in the course of the previous days.

The camping tradition concluded in 2012 when Camp Mensch Mill was sold to the Amitabha Buddhist Society of Philadelphia. There was much anguish and resentment when the conference voted by a very slight margin of three votes to end a hundred-year tradition. Some felt that it was an abrogation of its responsibility to care for and preserve a holy place. However, the only constant in the universe is change, and newer generations will find other opportunities and places for spiritual formation and human fellowship. It is significant that the church camp was sold to a Buddhist organization, since Buddhism teaches the importance of recognizing the impermanence of all things, and that in order to avoid suffering we must free ourselves from all attachments.

Life does move on, but the memories endure, and we can take comfort in that. Fred Wentzel had many memories of the camp, even after just a few years. On a train to Chicago, he began writing a poem that he completed in a small, crowded room of a Chicago YMCA. The poem was set to the music of Fritz Kreisler's "The Old Refrain" and became the camp song.

> I often think of you, O glad Mensch Mill,
> Your friendships deep and dear, your far-viewed Hill
> Where silence whispers low and God comes near,
> Where souls are freed by love that knows no fear.
> I walk your laughing paths, your quiet wood,
> And dream of times that know no law but good.
> O may my ways be fair and bravely right,
> Clean as your morning sun, calm as your night.
> I see your lights grow dim, your candles glow,
> High stars through trees above, bright fires below;
> My heart is full of you, O gracious Mill,
> O friends whose hands are true, O far-viewed Hill.

The High Meadow

Thomas Maybury was the inventor of the first cookstove in America. A stone replica marks the location of his forge in Hereford Township, Pennsylvania, which became the site of a church camp. The monument had been my favorite spot for the dawn meditation known as "morning watch" overlooking the pond at Camp Mensch Mill.

The entire area was steeped in local history as the site of several mills over the centuries, but it was Maybury that fascinated me. Before it became a museum piece, his cast iron stove sat on the first floor of Adam Mensch's house, later a girl's dormitory, and a convenient place to stash contraband food taken from the dining hall a few yards away. The legend is that when Maybury died in 1747, his Lenni Lenape friends carried his body to a wooded area next to a high meadow. Only a few campers knew the location of the grave and how to get there. It was not well visited, just as his Native American neighbors expected.

Summer camp was also a place for falling in love and exploring the first running of adolescent hormones. I didn't realize it at first, but like the salmon that is drawn to its place of origin by an irresistible and inherent urge, I also returned each summer. Yes, it was a place of community, a place in which you knew you belonged and were accepted, where you could discover the natural world and the mysterious aspects of your own psyche and your relationship with God, but it was also a place to discover the mysteries of the opposite sex.

Diane was one of these summer romances that I thought would fade at the conclusion of the camp session. It was the year that I had decided to remain for a second session and was surprised when she visited me on a

Sunday afternoon. During the two-week camps, Sundays were fairly open, allowing time for families to come and see what was going on. Diane and I would not be missed, so we hiked the high hill to find Mayberry's grave.

After we paid our respects at the small stone marker in the woods, we paused for a momentary embrace in the high meadow. The moment of passion had no chance to develop. A sudden thunderstorm and soaking rain interrupted our intentions as we scurried down the hill, but I thought that it was the beginning of something wonderful.

During the autumn months, we corresponded and expressed our love for one another, eagerly anticipating our Christmas reunion. On the three-hour bus ride to Allentown, bearing a Christmas gift, I pondered what I would say to her after those months apart. But the moment had passed. We looked at each other, said little, and then she left. Waiting at the bus station for my return ride, someone put a quarter in the jukebox and played Johnny Mathis's song "The Twelfth of Never." It was one of the loneliest nights of my life.

I returned to the camp the next summer, my final year as a camper, and met my future wife. The camp director asked me to become a counselor at another camp a few weeks later and I accepted the assignment. When I carried my pack into Oaks Cabin at Camp Fernbook, I noticed that my co-counselor had a picture of Diane on the shelf by his bed.

Did I just show up at the wrong time and with the wrong girl? Was something going to happen, but I arrived earlier? How long does the inevitable take? Are there moments when something is ripe to occur—the *kairos* moment when you realize that this is what is destined to be?

While in college, I stopped by to see Diane. Her mother said that she was away. I took this as one more sign that the relationship was not meant to be. Life consists of doors opening and slamming shut, and other doors opening with different options and opportunities. One could go through life waiting for things to happen, or *carpe diem*, make them happen. Either way, life is unfolding as it should and the process moves inexorably to its own conclusion.

Alliene

———

At Camp Mensch Mill there is a tree planted years ago to honor Alliene DeChant. It is next to the dining hall and I see it often when I visit the camp, and I think of the other trees that were planted many years ago when Alliene first came to this place that so many of us hold dear. How much like a tree are our own lives. Our roots go deep into our heritage as we draw nourishment from our family, our traditions and values, our faith in God, and our love for our brothers and sisters. They are all part of the rich soil that enables us to grow and shapes our future. Though firmly rooted, a person, like a tree, can send their branches skyward and outward and reach beyond the place assigned to them

Born of home-missionary parents in the heartland of America, Alliene grew up in Abilene, Kansas, a childhood contemporary of Dwight Eisenhower, and where she campaigned for Woodrow Wilson. Her rootage was in the pioneer and pilgrim spirit that led her to the distant corners of the world to follow in the footsteps of Gandhi and Schweitzer; to touch the lives of thousands of people, young and old; to have experiences that most of us only read about; to have the love and support from her family, which she returned in full measure. The writer of the Letter to the Hebrews says of the Old Testament pioneers of faith, "These all died in faith . . . and confessed that they were strangers and pilgrims on the earth" (Hebrews 11:13). Alliene wrote about her pilgrimage in her book *I Came This Way*.

Miss DeChant was a member of my church in Kutztown. She was proud of her Huguenot background and felt at home among others of the French Reformed tradition who had fled France to escape persecution. She became editor of our hometown newspaper. When I first met Alliene, she was living in a nursing home. I would visit her often and we had long conversations before her dementia increased. But oh the stories she would tell.

She was a graduate of Hood College in Maryland, one of our Evangelical and Reformed schools, and then embarked on a lifelong journey filled with adventure and experiences that would fill many lifetimes. She traveled by plane and cargo steamer to Japan, China, Burma, India, Africa, Palestine, and the European countries. From Rangoon to Mandalay, in Itaunja, a village of the untouchables, at the foot of Mt. Everest, up the Yangtze, on the Via Dolorosa, from the World Council of Churches in Evanston to the Cotswolds of England, Alliene had been there. She taught school in Japan and China. She was a Girl Scout leader and knew Juliette Lowe, its founder. She was a camp counselor, missionary, teacher, newspaper reporter, editor, and so much more. The books she wrote reflect her life: *I Came This Way, Of the Dutch I Sing, Down Oley Way, Seedtime and Harvest.*

A short time after meeting Alliene, I mentioned that when I graduated from high school, my pastor, Daniel Schlinkmann, who also happened to be from the same Midwest area as Alliene, had given me a book entitled *Out of My Heart: A Pastor's Diary*, by Clement W. DeChant. Having the same last name, I asked her if they were related. Indeed, they were. Clement was Alliene's brother, and he had included some poems that he had written upon the death of their father. I used one of Clem's poems at Alliene's funeral. Alliene had given me the autographed copy of her brother's book.

Alliene died in September of 1982. I scattered her ashes on Vesper Hill at Mensch Mill, a place she loved so much and where she influenced so many young people. She bequeathed to me her Revised Standard Version Bible, which she had read cover to cover at least three times and apparently consulted many more times. It was heavily underlined by a woman who not only studied it well, but lived by its precepts.

There are people who wander through this world with no idea of where they are going. They have no idea of what their purpose in life is, and so they do not know what roads to take. There are others who know where they are going and know how to get there. They know why they have been created and what their purpose for being is all about.

Albert Einstein wrote of the purpose of life:

> How extraordinary is the situation of us mortals. Each of us is here for a brief sojourn; for what purpose he knows not, though he sometimes thinks he senses it. But without going deeper than our daily life, it is plain that we exist for our fellow-men-in the

first place for those upon whose smiles and welfare our happiness depends . . . and next for all those unknown to us personally but to whose destinies we are bound by the tie of sympathy. A hundred times every day I remind myself that my inner and outer life depend on the labors of other men, living and dead, all that I must exert myself in order to be given in the measure as I have received and am still receiving.[1]

Most of us are born for the purpose of learning and spiritual growth through dealing with some adversity of life, or overcoming a defect of our character, or by hearing the pains and agonies of others. And then there are a few who have the added purpose of life to be a light and a help to others. Alliene DeChant achieved greatness among us not by what she received, but by what she gave. She taught us by her experiences that our system of values should measure a person's worth not by what one accumulates in life, but by what one gives to others.

My last visits to Alliene at the Lutheran Home at Topton were during the time that her consciousness had diminished and her awareness of our reality grew dimmer. But locked within her soul was the memory of loving and devoted service to her church, to her community, and to thousands of persons in this world and the next. As her spirit slipped the surly bonds of earth and soared to freedom in the heavenly realms, I knew that she was more alive than ever she had been on earth. We bury our hopes or scatter them to the wind only that God may resurrect them to new life and rekindle the flame that it may illumine other worlds.

Lines on a Hope Abandoned
by Clement W. DeChant
read at Alliene's funeral

A light went out!
It was a brave, clean flame.

It flickered long,

As candle gutters in its final pool of wax,
Hoping to keep on burning even brighter than before.

I took the lifeless stuff that once was flame;
And tenderly, I wrapped It soft and warm
Against the Winter's cold, and snow, and rain,
I made a narrow box to lay it in —

---

1. Einstein, "World as I See It," from an essay originally published in *Forum and Century* 84 (1931) 193–94.

Fine wood and workmanship, and carved with tears.
Sexton and priest,
I buried It at night beneath the apple tree,
Where orioles,
To share my grief, come singing in the spring.[2]

---

2. DeChant, *Out of My Heart*, 130.

Tapestry

There are more than eight billion people living on this planet at the present time. In our own lifetimes each of us will come in contact with a mere fraction of that number. We may remember the names of a few thousand, and those who have a direct influence on our lives may number in the hundreds. Yet the intersection of every one of those lives with our own changes us, however slightly, and in the aggregate we become different people.

Carl Jung coined the term "synchronicity" to refer to seemingly unrelated events, disconnected by time or place, that produce a convergence and affect the destiny of the world. Nothing is accidental. Seemingly incidental experiences of our lives and the world around us have an ultimate purpose. Like billiard balls careening haphazardly on a table, colliding with others with sufficient force to alter the trajectory of both, or brushing ever so closely to others as to hardly effect a change in position, so the people and events of our lives modify who we are and what we are destined to become.

Obviously the cataclysmic events of September 11, 2001 have dramatically altered the way we live, and how nations and peoples relate to one another. Examining in detail the lives lost and the lives saved, we would find extraordinary stories of persons being in the right or wrong place at a particular moment that either saved or doomed them. A missed flight, a sudden illness, a pause in a daily routine—any number of minor or major distractions preceding the tragedy could have produced a cascading effect that has changed thousands of lives forever.

Incidental decisions can alter the course of one's life in astounding ways, to the point where one wonders if the decision really was incidental or a part of a larger design. When I was ten years old, my Sunday school teacher encouraged me to write for a stewardship promotion contest offered each year by the denomination. First prize was an all-expense-paid vacation at a church-operated resort in Pennsylvania, courtesy of St. Stephan's Church. It was really a ploy to get city kids to take advantage of the church camping program. I won and I went.

My counselor at Camp Fernbrook was a senior seminary student named Bruce Hatt, a kind and wonderful man with a great sense of humor who was great with kids. We teased Bruce about his flirtation with a kitchen girl, Millie, whom he would later marry. I had no way of knowing how this one-week experience would become a strand weaving itself into the fabric of my life. It was a mountaintop event from which I did not want to descend.

I returned for a second and third year at Fernbook. Bruce was no longer there, but my counselor both years was also a seminarian, Bob Reiff, who also fell in love with and eventually married a kitchen girl, named Betty. As I later learned, Betty and Millie were sisters. There was a third sister, Marie, who also married a minister with whom I worked at camp, and their brother, George Yoder, was also a pastor.

Prior to the merger that resulted in the United Church of Christ, the camps I attended, Fernbrook and Mensch Mill, were operated by an intersynodal board representing nine synods in Pennsylvania, New Jersey, and New York, more than a thousand local congregations. The staff, however, was drawn from all over the country. The camps were a virtually breeding ground for future church leaders, and for the husbands and wives that they found there. One staff member, detecting some interest in ministry in a chance remark I had made, sent me some brochures after the camp session ended. It was one of the nudges that God gives when God wants you to move in a particular direction. A few years later, when I decided to apply for "in-care status," indicating intent to pursue a Christian vocation, the chair of the Ministry Committee happened to be the father of the pastor who offered that first encouragement. He appointed a minister from Irvington, New Jersey to be my mentor.

Ron Keller was different from most ministers I had come to know. He maintained a high liturgical tradition, and always wore a Roman collar to match his strong sense of ecclesiology and ritual. It was rumored that even his pajamas had a clerical collar. I liked his style, especially his open sports car and red scarf. I had hoped to learn much from him, but he soon left our association and took a church in Pennsylvania.

Ron was succeeded by George Shults, a saintly man who saw only the good in people and was embarrassed if one of his observations was misconstrued as being overly critical. George served a mission church in mid-Jersey. I worked with his son, Bob, traveling the state to set up, develop, and strengthen local youth programs in UCC churches.

During my senior year in seminary, I received a call from Bruce Hatt, who asked me to be his associate director at Mensch Mill. Bruce had recently resigned as pastor of St. John's Church in Kutztown to become executive director for the camps whose offices were located in the church he had served. Called as the new pastor for St. John's was my friend and mentor George Shults. At one of the summer camping sessions was Bob Reiff, who had left Zion Church, Womelsdorf, to become a missionary to Japan.

One would think that I was moving in a very tight circle of clergy friends and associates, and yet the two pastoral changes that I would make appeared to be more than coincidence. After four years at my first parish, a very small congregation in Martin Creek, Pennsylvania, I moved to Womelsdorf, where Bob Reiff had been, and within six years I would succeed Bruce and George at Kutztown. Unable to find housing in that university town, we bought a house in nearby Fleetwood, only to discover that Ron Keller lived on the same street. Coincidences would compound when, several years later, the daughter of two of my Mensch Mill counselors, Nevin and Clare, now pastor of the Fleetwood church, moved in a few doors away.

While there were many more striking coincidences and mergings of parallel paths, they only contributed to the perception that there seemed to be some design to the way my life was playing out. It was as if all of us had gotten together before we were born and decided how we would interact with each other. While some have had more influence than others, and a few have been only incidental contacts of short, though repeated, duration, I cannot help but see some overall plan. Perhaps it is a natural human instinct to seek to impose order upon the universe and to seek connections where none exist.

However, the more we learn about our fragile ecosystems and see how all of life impacts upon the whole, I am convinced that God does not play at dice and that what appears to be random and coincidental are simply pieces of the puzzle that have not yet been placed into the larger picture.

Synchronicity

A lot of seeds fall into our lives and not all of them take root, and much is seemingly wasted, but collectively they affect us, often in ways we never realize at the time. In Robert H. Hopcke's book *There Are No Accidents*, the author, a psychotherapist, describes the Jungian concept of synchronicity. Synchronicity is those haunting and meaningful coincidences that we all experience, those moments when events conspire to tell us something significant is happening.

For example, I was once invited to present a paper at an academic conference in Philadelphia. The group was international in scope, with professors, researchers, physicians, and scientists from all over the world—India, Holland, Canada, Texas, Hawaii, United Kingdom, Florida, and so on. I was one of eleven presenters at the conference.

The night before the final session, in which the last two papers would be read, one of which was mine, I had dinner with a few of the academy members, including the woman who would immediately precede me the next day. In the course of conversation, I discovered not only that she came from the same city that I did, but that she grew up two blocks from me and went to the same school and knew the same teachers. She knew of my uncle's art studio and had expressed a desire to visit it.

I suppose someone somewhere could figure out the mathematical odds of such an event occurring, but what is most astounding is that these synchronous events or coincidences occur quite frequently to all of us. We often say, "Isn't that amazing," and then move on with the rest of our lives.

What we ought to do is see what these stories or coincidences are trying to tell us about our lives, our future, our destiny according to God's plans for us.

I was in a bookstore in Kutztown for the first time when the owner gave me a book that she thought I might be interested in. The store sells both new and used books that people bring in. She wasn't able to sell this used book, because it was a handwritten dream journal. I accepted the book, and when I looked into it, discovered that it was written by Frances Brooks, whom I had known some fifty years ago. Her family lived twenty-five miles away, and when Frances died, her daughter brought her books to Kutztown. Frances was born in London and had an interest in the occult. Her dreams had a vague familiarity to me. With me in the store at the time was Dale Graff, a researcher into dreams and precognition.

This was just one of those random events that occur with great frequency that we dismiss as mere coincidence. Shortly after this incident, I received an email from a man whom I had as a confirmation class student some twenty years ago, and had lost touch with since. He is now a medical student and was working on a Native American Hoopa reservation in California. He said that he was accompanying Dr. Mark Rader, a very close friend of mine, on his rounds. They did not know each other prior to their meeting. While anomalous, it is not all that unusual in the grand scheme of things.

On the other hand, there may be a causal relationship that is yet to be determined. In Jesus' Parable of the Sower, the distribution of seed is somewhat haphazard. The seed falls all over the place: some of it on paths where birds devour it, some of it on rocky ground where it is parched by the sun, some of it amidst thorns that choke it, and some of it in good soil where it takes root and grows.

Perhaps the sower is God and the seeds are possibilities for the growth of the awareness of God among humans.

We may wonder: Why bother to have church services in summer when only a few show up? Why bother to contribute to missions to help people we don't know or who may not appreciate it? Why bother providing hospitality to a refugee family who is not of our faith? Why bother offering a kind word to a stranger who waits on us in a store or restaurant whom we may never see again? Why bother with random acts of kindness that seemingly will bear no fruit?

The answer is that we are not the judges either of the seed or of the soil. It is by God's design that the seed falls in the right places and that growth occurs. We are only called by God to share the good news of God's presence in a wasteful, inefficient manner, to embody the Christ spirit in every moment, in every place. If we only share it where sufficient people will receive it gladly, then we have neglected a part of our task. Instead of a reckless slinging of love and peace into the lives of all people, a kind of slinging that mirrors the nature of God, we might just dump the whole bag of seed where we think it will produce the greatest return on our investment. In doing so, we would be choosing who the select group is that we feel should receive the gospel. God doesn't work that way. God offers life to all.

Synchronous events, coincidences, chaos theory, unified field theory, and other expressions of events that boggle our minds only seem that way because the universe is still unfolding, and answers may not come until it has all played out. Our consciousness is limitless, but only when it melds with the consciousness of God will we truly understand.[1]

---

1. For more on the nature of universal consciousness, see my book *The Mysticism of Ordinary and Extraordinary Experience*.

It's About Time

My Volga German grandparents spoke to each other in German, especially when they didn't want us kids to know what was going on. While I never became as fluent in German as I would have liked, I did manage to learn a few expressions. My grandfather was the embodiment of Germanic order and precision. Meals had to be served precisely at their appointed time and certain rituals had to be observed. He would ask my grandmother, "*Was ist die Uhr?*"—literally, "What is the clock (or hour)?" He knew what time it was, but it was his way of telling her that she had better get his dinner ready.

I learned that the Germans are like the Greeks in that they have two ways of asking about the time. "*Was ist die Uhr?*" is if you want to know what the clock says. But if you have somewhere to go, or something to do, or are waiting for something to happen, you ask, "*Wie spät ist es?*"—"How late is it?" How much time is left before the appointed hour?

We might ask that question in terms of our life's journey. How much time do we have left before we punch the clock? How much time does the world have before Armageddon comes?

Jesus said we don't know, and cannot know. Only God knows. But we should be prepared. One humorous rendition of the old nursery rhyme says, "Hickory, dickory, dock. Two mice ran up the clock. The clock struck one, and the other one got away."

> Then two will be in the field; one will be taken and one will be left. Two women will be grinding meal together; one will be taken and one will be left. Keep awake therefore, for you do not know on what day your Lord is coming. . . . Therefore you also must be

ready, for the Son of Man is coming at an unexpected hour. (Matthew 24:40–44)

I wonder how many of those who boarded the Titanic knew that they would not complete the journey. I wonder if any of the parents who send their children to school expect that they might not return and become victims of the many mass shootings. Who will die and who will live? Most people never know when their last day will come. Jesus' advice is to be ready every day.

Evan T. Pritchard has written a book entitled *No Word for Time*.[1] Pritchard, who is part Native American, tells us that the Algonquin people do not have a word for time; they live in a world without clocks. They have learned that the way to be happy is to always allow for each task the time necessary to complete it fully. Things get done in the time they need to be done. When part of you is watching the time, you are not present to the moment. A clock is never in the present moment. The key to happiness is to see eternity in this moment of time. The sacred is a present reality as well as a future hope.

It is the nature of humans to define, to impose limits, to see a conclusion. A Sunday school child asks, "How old is God?" and the teacher is baffled. We want to know when the universe began. Archbishop James Ussher in the seventeenth century calculated the date of creation to be October 22, 4004 BC, at 6:00 p.m. And thousands of apocalypticists have ventured dates for the second coming of Christ and the end of time. These are impossible questions that defy rational answers.

Macbeth was right on when he pondered:

> Tomorrow, and tomorrow, and tomorrow,
> Creeps in this petty pace from day to day,
> To the last syllable of recorded time;
> And all our yesterdays have lighted fools
> The way to dusty death. Out, out, brief candle!
> Life's but a walking shadow, a poor player,
> That struts and frets his hour upon the stage,
> And then is heard no more. It is a tale
> Told by an idiot, full of sound and fury,
> Signifying nothing.[2]

---

1. Pritchard, *No Word for Time*, 11–19.
2. *Macbeth*, act 5, scene 5.

Of course, Macbeth was bothered by the futility of life and the meaninglessness of existence, as exemplified by the murder of Duncan. Had he adopted a more existential philosophy, he may not have found himself in a quandary. His soliloquy is a reaction to the news of his wife's death, and perhaps we can detect a bit of karmic "reap what you sow" payback.

It may be that life is a never-ending laboratory of constant experiments, and that at some point we will realize that the only element of importance in the universe is love, and that after we are done strutting and fretting we will be enveloped by the love of God.

During times of great calamity and death, people fear the end of time, the destruction of the world, when God will roll up the heavens like a scroll and bring human existence to its necessary conclusion.

Jesus also referred to the end times when one of the disciples asked about the city of Jerusalem. He said, "Do you see these great buildings? Not one stone will be left here upon another; all will be thrown down." That actually happened forty years later when the Romans destroyed the city. But Jesus went on to say:

> When you hear of wars and rumors of wars, do not be alarmed; this must take place, but the end is still to come. For nation will rise against nation, and kingdom against kingdom; there will be earthquakes in various places; there will be famines. This is but the beginning of the birth pangs. (Mark 13:7–8)

Christians have expected the end of existence periodically, when time shall be no more. They expected it during Nero's persecution of the church, during persecutions under Diocletian and other emperors, in 410 when Rome was burned by the Visigoths, during the time of the Black Death in the thirteenth century, and during the wars of religion in the sixteenth and seventeenth centuries, when our forebears came to this area to build the New Jerusalem in the promised land of Pennsylvania. The Jehovah's Witnesses made so many predictions about the end of the world during the last century that they have finally given up on setting a date.

Jesus said that no one knows when the end will come, so it's hard to understand why there are so many Christians who believe we are living in the end times. There is even a website that contains a "Rapture Index" that gives daily odds on how close we are to the second coming.

I think it is important for us to understand the nature of reality and the purpose of human existence. We take such a narrow view of life that we tend to judge life by our own slice of existence, and not by God's greater plan for us. In fact, there are more people today than ever before who have a difficult time believing in God at all. What pushes them to their conclusions are the various expressions of the world's religions that have sanctioned the worst kinds of inhumane behavior and cruelty in the name of God. Richard Dawkins, a preeminent scientist and prominent atheist, has written a book called *The God Delusion*, in which he mounts an attack against the religious concept of God and the harm it has inflicted on the human race. He would not have an argument from me about the way religion has been misinterpreted and misused, but he cannot explain the very idea of existence, the *why* of our being, without God.

Before the creation of the universe, there was God. When the universe ceases to exist, there will be God. We used to conclude many of our prayers with the words "world without end," to indicate that God transcends time and space, that God is without beginning or ending. If we really believe that we have been called into being as persons by God, and infused with the spirit of God, it is reasonable to assume that the spirit within us is also without end. *There is no conclusion, only change.* The world as we know it may come to an end, but we do not. We will continue to grow spiritually as we learn from our mistakes and move forward.

Sometimes it takes a long time to learn, and the lessons have to be repeated over and over again until we get it. It is important for us to get a larger perspective on the meaning of life than simply our own little fragment of our time on this planet.

Let me try to frame this in another way. We don't always understand why things happen the way they do. People may say things that wound us deeply and inflict emotional scars on our psyches that last a lifetime, and then all of a sudden there is an epiphany and we understand the *why* of our pain.

An old Johnny Mathis song, "The Twelfth of Never," is about how long love will last. It concludes with this line: "Until the twelfth of never and that's a long, long time."

The twelfth of never is chronological time that does not end, but yet the words of the song speak of love that does not end, and therefore it is about *kairos* time, what the Greeks referred to as time that has meaning, time that is fulfilled. It is the time of God in which we accomplish our reason for being.

Jesus said that there is no conclusion, only change. The world's ending is but the birth pangs of a new creation, and we will continue to the twelfth of never until we not only learn the meaning of love, but that love pervades all that is and will be. For God is love itself.

You Can't Go Home Again

Thomas Wolfe, in his final novel, *You Can't Go Home Again*, has George Webber returning to America from his travels abroad only to find that he can't go home again, because home no longer exists. The past has become the present. Time, like the river, has moved on. We are all searching for the past because we are familiar with it; we are secure in it because we know how it turned out. But it would not have turned out the way it did unless we had left, unless we had changed and made a difference. There would be no Christianity today had the disciples refused to leave their past. The world has changed because they changed, and they could never go back to what was because they had changed their world.

We once referred to the "me generation," the baby boomers, who were so caught up in their own egos and selfish pursuits for affluence and selfgratification. Whatever happened to them? They didn't disappear—they changed. They matured into a generation concerned with spiritual discovery, who are now willing to reach out and commit themselves to something of importance, yearning for relationships and connections, longing for more stable anchors in their lives. This new generation of seekers is looking to Christ, not just because of a vision that he had two thousand years ago, but because of the new vision that his spirit brings to our world today.

Years ago, T. S. Eliot wrote about Little Gidding, a small village that had provided refuge for Nicholas Ferrar in 1625, only to be destroyed during the English Civil War. Eliot was writing in 1942 after London had survived the Blitz and was looking forward to rebuilding. Life is an endless cycle of birth and rebirth, during which we experience all that we can. It most certainly is the journey that is important, not the destination, for the destination is where we have started. But when we return to the beginning, we are not the same person, and our new home is where we begin again.

Thomas Wolfe's book *You Can't Go Home Again* was published posthumously. The last two paragraphs of the book appear to be a prophecy of his approaching death, but in another sense the words speak of leaving behind the past for a larger vision of tomorrow.

> Something has spoken to me in the night, burning the tapers of the waning year; something has spoken in the night, and told me I shall die, I know not where. Saying:
> "To lose the earth you know, for greater knowing; to lose the life you have, for greater life; to leave the friends you loved, for greater loving; to find a land more kind than home, more large than earth
> —Whereon the pillars of this earth are founded, toward which the conscience of the world is tending— a wind is rising, and the rivers flow."[1]

That's what the disciples did. That's what we need to do. The future awaits us. Let's move in the right direction. As Thomas Wolfe said, we cannot go home again, because the past no longer exists, but we should not be looking back for the wrong reason. The problem is not so much in looking back on the past to see how far you have come, but in looking back with longing to relive the past. The rest of my life is going to be spent in the future. Nothing is gained by turning back except to check my progress.

Since I graduated from high school, I have returned to those hallowed halls only once. It was my first visit in more than thirty years. There was only one teacher remaining that I had had as a student and she was going to retire the following year. She asked me what brought me back, and I told her that I wanted to see if Thomas Wolfe was right. "He was right," she said. "You can't go home again." Nothing was the same anymore. I knew that, of course, the moment I stepped through the door. Not only had the building changed, but the students were different, of different ethnic composition. Security guards had replaced hall monitors, and one had to pass through metal detectors. The bilingual posters indicated a different educational method. This was not the school I had known.

You cannot step into the same river twice, for time is an ever-flowing stream and moves away from each moment.

---

1. Wolfe, *You Can't Go Home Again*, 638.

Jesus told a parable that leads us to believe that you *can* go home again. The Prodigal Son returned to the open arms of a loving father. But in another sense, he could never return home—not to the home he left. Because he was now a different person. His relationship to his father and to his brother was not the same. His values were different. His perspective on life had changed. Even if his house remained the same and his father and brother had not aged, it would have been different because he was different. You cannot go home again. You cannot turn back to life as it was, because the purpose of life is to learn and to point you to the future. Those who seek to turn back are doomed.

One of the most pathetic stories in Greek mythology is that of Orpheus and Eurydice. Orpheus, a great musician and singer, was deeply in love with the beautiful Eurydice and was devastated when she died young. He prayed that the gods might restore her to life, but his words were to no avail. He was willing to travel to Hades, the realm of the dead, in an effort to bring her back.

Descending into the depths, haunted by the spirits of the dead, Orpheus came before the throne of Pluto, the dreaded god of the underworld. Orpheus played his lyre and sang such a sad lament that even Pluto took pity. Summoning Eurydice, he gave her to Orpheus and told him that he could return to the land of the living. However, he imposed one condition. Orpheus was to lead the way, but if he should look back even once, Eurydice would return to Hades.

Orpheus accepted the condition and began his ascent to the upper world. Unfortunately, as he approached the light, he was overcome by doubt and turned slightly to see if Eurydice was still with him. In that one brief moment, Eurydice faded from his grasp and was lost forever.

The Greeks told this myth to show that doubt has its consequences and that one must not look back to the past. Looking back for lack of faith, Orpheus lost his beloved Eurydice.

Jesus, in the same way, hit on the admonition not to look back again. "No one who puts his hand to the plow and looks back is fit for the kingdom of God" (Luke 9:62). The future is before you. That is the image that must be fresh in our minds. Not the stale images of the past, but the fresh vision we have gained from all the days of our living.

Plus Ultra

Mary Herbine's continual retelling of her father's death on Christmas Eve and hearing the carolers outside her home singing "Joy to the World" is just one example of the incongruity and irony of life, of hearing the sound of joy in the midst of grief.

The 1662 Anglican *Book of Common Prayer* Burial Service has the phrase, "In the Midst of Life, We Are in Death." There is no way to avoid the inevitable finality of life, which intrudes into our most joyous celebrations of life. Death, it seems, is always in the air. Our family waited for the conclusion of life for a beloved uncle. A resident of a nursing home who had resisted for years leaving his home told me in the midst of his depression, "This is it. Nobody gets out of here alive." He saw the nursing facility as a terminal to wait for his final journey. "Terminal" is a good word for it. Death is indeed the last enemy that we face.

A member of my church who rarely attended worship had suffered a heart attack. When I went to visit him, he was reading the family Bible. I casually asked him if he was "cramming for the finals." He smiled and said, "I just want to know what to expect."

We want happy endings in life. Feel-good movies and situational comedies are always more popular than dramas that force us to confront our own mortality. When we watch melodramas, it is always with the belief that it will never happen to us. Good Friday will never draw the crowds that Easter does. The darkness of noon at Golgotha can never match the brilliant dawn in the garden of the empty tomb.

The question that is continually before us in the practice of our religion is: Are we responding because of fear or because of faith? Do we avoid bringing death into our consciousness, our conversation, because we are afraid of it? Or have we transcended death and recognized that it no longer holds any power over us because it has been defeated by Jesus on the cross? When you whistle in the cemetery at night, is it because of fear or because of faith?

Centuries ago in England, mazes were constructed with many sharp turns, false passages, and virtually no extended straight lines because witches can't turn corners. Witches have to fly in straight lines. To avoid evil, one would enter a maze and try to lose the forces of darkness that were pursuing you. One could get lost in a maze.

The labyrinth, on the other hand, was constructed in the medieval church to be a metaphor for the spiritual journey. In the labyrinth, the paths were curved and often doubled back on each other, but there was only one direction, and inevitably you would find your center. The lesson that the medieval Christian learned was that by following the path of faith, you eventually attain your salvation and a paradise of eternal life in the presence of God.

Somehow, there are many in our culture that have entered the maze instead of the labyrinth and have gotten lost. We believe that the only reality is the one we are now experiencing. We are not looking for the eternal life of the spirit; we want eternal life now by avoiding death at all costs.

We have succeeded in extending biological life far beyond what most people could expect a few centuries ago. But the life of the mind and the life of the spirit have some catching up to do. Visit our nursing homes and see how many persons are now in the dementia units. Their bodies have lived beyond their minds. And how many of our elderly are so bored with living that they pray for a peaceful death? A woman in her nineties once said to me that "getting old isn't easy." I said that it wasn't so bad when you consider the alternative. And she quickly replied, "I'm not so sure about that anymore."

I learned a while back that many gen-Xers and millennials, those born since 1970, had started cosmetic surgery Health Savings Accounts while in their twenties. They wanted to be ready to avoid looking their age when they reached fifty and beyond. Such cosmetic surgery, I'm told, is a booming industry, even without insurance coverage. They won't admit to growing old, much less to dying. Does anyone doubt that the young today will force cosmetic surgery to be considered normal health care and covered by health insurance? "Lifestyle medicine," as it's called, will be as important to those now under fifty as is the current life-prolonging medicine is today. Young people are expecting that replacement body parts will be standard medicine as they age and wear out their original equipment. For the young, death is no longer cool. For example, we don't like movies in which the hero or heroine dies at the end. Such films usually bomb at the box office.

Notice how in many of the movies in the last fifty years that deal with death, people don't actually die. This is no accident. *Buffy the Vampire Slayer* features Buffy and her boyfriend, Angel, who just won't die. Then there is *Meet Joe Black*, an interminable movie about the delayed termination of a tycoon. *In What Dreams May Come*, Robin Williams is killed in a car crash but incredibly reunited with wife, kids, and the family dog. Even *Titanic* features Jack and Rose happy after all, despite Jack's drowning, reunited on the grand staircase as if the whole iceberg thing had just been a Hollywood set. Some viewers were very upset that in the film *One True Thing* Meryl Streep actually dies of cancer and really leaves her daughter behind. We are convinced that death will not be, for us at least, a dead end.

The problem with this is that it has nothing to do with our biblical faith and with the Easter story. Jesus really died. He did not appear to die. He was not asleep. He died a death more cruel and painful than we can imagine. He wasn't dead for a moment on the operating room table having an out-of-body experience. He was dead, sealed in the grave for three days. The disciples did not deceive themselves about his death, did not have a sense that though he was crucified, "he will live on in our memories or pop back up in our dreams." The one whom they loved, in whom they had hoped, was dead. They came to the tomb in great grief. When they saw that the tomb was empty, they didn't think, "Jesus is immortal." They thought, "Somebody stole his body." There's a lot of weeping, of real grief in the story as John tells it in his gospel. Tears are the appropriate response to the reality, the finality, the totality of death, as we well know.

Yet, within a few days, Jesus's followers began to understand that what had happened to him was "according to the Scriptures." That is, Israel believed that one day God was going to solve the problem of Israel's suffering and oppression and, while God was at it, God would solve the problem of evil and injustice in all the world. The Scriptures promised such a day of divine victory. On Easter, the disciples discovered this victory in the resurrection of Jesus. The cross, which they had thought was the end, the death of their relationship with Jesus, was really the beginning.

Kahlil Gibran, in his masterpiece book of poetry, *The Prophet*, wrote: "if you would know the secret of death, you must seek it in the heart of life. . . In the depths of your hopes and desires lies your silent knowledge of the beyond. And like the seeds beneath the snow, your heart dreams of spring. Trust your dreams, your faith, for in them is hidden the gate to eternity."[1]

Death was never the real enemy. It is the fear of death. As Jesus conquered death, so faith conquers fear. We know that we shall live and be raised to a new life. The God who created you and breathed life into your body will not permit that flame to be extinguished forever. As John Donne wrote in "Holy Sonnet 10":

> One short sleep past, we wake eternally,
> And Death shall be no more: Death, thou shalt die!

"The last enemy to be destroyed is death" (1 Corinthians 15:26). And in God's time, that has already occurred.

The Pillars of Hercules at the western end of the Mediterranean Sea marked the limits of the ancient world. A marker was placed at the Strait of Gibraltar with the words in Latin, *NE PLUS ULTRA*—"Nothing More Beyond." Then Columbus discovered a new world, and Balboa stood upon a peak in Darien and viewed both the Atlantic and Pacific Oceans, the familiar and the undiscovered. The marker at Gibraltar was changed to read *PLUS ULTRA*—"More Beyond."

It is a faith that I accept. There is so much more beyond. The last barrier has been removed and we go forward into new adventures.

---

1. Gibran, *Prophet*, 80.

Latin Class

At Ursinus College I was a history major with a classics minor. I had thirty-three semester hours with one professor, Donald Baker. Sometimes the entire class consisted of just two people. I didn't learn as much Latin and Greek as I did about how to live and confront spiritual seeking. Dr. Baker exuded a certain quietness and was often quite willing to pursue his own and his students' curiosity. Many class sessions were spent discussing contemporary culture instead of classical antiquity. A Harvard-educated Quaker, he reminded me of Mr. Chips, because he was more interested in sharing values rather than teaching a subject.

When I visited him years later at his home on Contention Pond in New Hampshire (how the name of that lake suited him), I apologized on behalf of his students for leading him off topic. He, however, corrected me and said that history, particularly that of ancient Greece, still gives meaning and insight into our lives today. He taught us to be passionate about the things that were important to us, to raise a ruckus about matters of national and social relevance, to welcome the interchange of ideas and value the opinions of others without shifting with the wings of change, to be patient with the world, and taught us that there is more than material things that we should leave to our children and their children. These were the good legacies of the Graeco-Roman world and the teachings of Jesus.

I am not sure why we studied Ovid's *Ars Amatoria* (*The Art of Love*). This epic work may be good Latin and filled with practical advice on finding the right wife (or husband), engaging in dinner conversation, caring for one's spouse, as well as choosing a good aphrodisiac and arousing jealousy in one's partner. Of course, this work is studied in many college

Latin courses, but it is interesting that it was burned in Florence in 1497 by Savonarola, an early puritanical reformer. An English translation was confiscated by United States Customs in 1930.

Greeks like Socrates, Plato, Aristotle, in various settings such as the Academy and Symposia (literally, "with drink"), sat down together to discuss philosophy and politics and how they understood the gods speaking to them.

I often attended Friends meetings in Phoenixville with Dr. Baker. We sat in silence for a few minutes until someone felt moved to speak as he or she was moved by the Inner Light. Apparently, on a particular day that I attended, God had a lot to communicate, since there was little silence, but considerable discussion.

Sitting on his porch overlooking Contention Pond, I noticed copies of Emerson and Thoreau, which Dr. Baker must have read several times. Our conversation was interrupted by periods of silence, but the greater intrusion was the sound of an outboard motor shattering the quietness of the tranquil setting. He bemoaned the fact that this loud expression of civilization, if you could call it that, had come to his place of retreat. The barbarians were at the gates, and blessed quietness was becoming increasingly difficult to appropriate.

In my quest for quietness, I benefitted a bit more from a foreign student from Tibet. Lobsang Samden was the brother of the present Dalai Lama. He taught us much about sitting in silence and not thinking or seeking to bother God with so many questions. It is hard to be silent. It seems that God and I always have a lot to say to each other.

In my middle year at Lancaster Theological Seminary, I worked part-time as a Latin teacher at Edward Hand Junior High School. It is said that if you really want to know a subject, teach it to others. I am not sure that the first book of *Ars Amatoria* with its *cherchez la femme* instructions would have been that relevant to the ninth-grader who dropped my class because of pregnancy. We instead studied Julius Caesar's *Commentaries on the Gallic War*. It seemed more appropriate in this ghetto school, where gang fights were routine and I had to confiscate a switchblade from one of my students and stop fights in the hall.

We may study the past and its language, but unfortunately we don't always learn from it. The decline of the Roman Empire is sometimes attributed to their plumbing, whereby the use of leaded pipes and the extensive use of lead in many domestic items such as drinking cups had a deleterious effect on their heath, especially brain development. Only recently has modern science proven its harmful effects, in spite of one lead company advertising its health benefits.

However, we have learned some things from ancient Rome. We no longer use urine as a mouthwash to clean our teeth, or induce vomiting so that we can eat more at banquets. Our personal, social, and political practices change, and hopefully for the better. It is wise teachers who instill in us a desire to learn from the past that we might create a better future.

City of David

Long before Indiana Jones hit the big screen, I had career aspirations of becoming an archaeologist. I have always had a fascination for the ancient world and the archaeology that has brought much of it to light. As a young boy growing up in the New York area, the Metropolitan Museum of Art was a virtual alternate home, a cathedral of wonder, and a time machine to another world. The antiquities of Sumer, Egypt, Greece, and Rome were spellbinding and incited a lifelong interest in archaeology.

As a history major at Ursinus College, with a minor in classics, I had the opportunity to do my undergraduate thesis at the museum of the University of Pennsylvania on the royal tomb of Gordium in Anatolia, which gave me a window into Hittite culture. Having studied Latin and Greek, my real interest, however, was the Graeco-Roman world. I was grateful for the many visits to Italy and Greece to study these civilizations firsthand and to visit many archaeological sites.

My education at Lancaster Theological Seminary opened another dimension of interest, biblical archaeology, which I was able to pursue by participating in two digs in the Jerusalem area—the City of David and Ein Yael.

One usually associates the name Zion with the ancient city of Jerusalem, since it is a higher elevation and more readily defensible than some of the lower hills in the area, and at first glance it would seem most appropriate. Jerusalem, like Rome, is built on seven hills, three of which form the center of the old city: Moriah, the Temple Mount, where Abraham was asked to sacrifice his son, Isaac, and where Solomon built the first temple; Zion, the location of David's tomb and the site of the Last Supper, whose name came to be associated with the entire area; and Ophel, the lower spur that extends from the Temple Mount. It is on Mount Ophel where the ancient Jebusites built their city, primarily because of a water supply that was not available on Zion. David was able to breach the Jebusite defenses by sending Joab up the water shaft that supplied the city, a feat that earned him command of David's forces. Jebus thus became the City of David and the center of his power. Kathleen Kenyon had begun excavating the site from 1961 to 1967. She had been the most recent in a long line of archaeologists to work the site since 1863. Yigal Shiloh of Hebrew University resumed the work in 1978. I joined with other volunteers during the 1983 season, and last spoke with Professor Shiloh in 1985, shortly after he was diagnosed with stomach cancer. He died in 1987 at the age of fifty.

I arrived in Jerusalem after visiting with relatives in Italy and was booked at the Kings Hotel. I had requested the King David Hotel, but my agent either misunderstood or didn't know the difference. Kings was a rather dreary, somewhat boring accommodation in the New City, not far from the Ben Yehuda Mall, where several terrorist bombings have claimed the lives of nearly a hundred persons since 1948. It was not the kind of excitement I was looking for.

In the evening of my first day in Jerusalem, I took a walk to the Old City, entering Jaffa Gate. It was relatively quiet since most of the shops were closed, but I made my way to the Temple Mount area and the Western Wall. It is a strange feeling to be in such a storied land, with a history that stretches back to myth and conjures a truth that transcends the written record. I had never been interested in "walking where Jesus walked." I just wanted him to walk where I was walking. Yet, as I was to discover many times, there are sacred places that are infused with spiritual qualities that can be perceived beyond the normal sensory apparatus.

Retracing my steps to Jaffa Gate, I came upon Christ Church Hospice, across from the Citadel of David. They had a room available, and it was less expensive than the Kings Hotel, a shorter walk to the dig site, and a friendlier atmosphere. It was operated by the Anglican Church, presided over by a vicar who used a copious number of subjunctives when offering prayer, as if he didn't want to impose too much on the Almighty.

The archaeological site was a short walk past the Cardo, the Western Wall, through Dung Gate, and down a wide swale that had once been the Tyropean Valley, or Valley of the Cheesemakers, before the Romans filled it in with debris after their destruction of Jerusalem in 70 AD. The Tyropean

Valley separated Mount Zion from Ophel and the Lower City, which extended southward to the Pool of Siloam, just above where the Kidron Valley meets the Valley of Hinnom. Hinnom in biblical times was Gehenna, a place of tombs, lepers, and constantly burning fires consuming Jerusalem's trash. It was such a foreboding place that Jesus used it as a metaphor for hell. It was this interconnecting series of valleys that gave Jerusalem its strategic location and provided it with a secure defensive position on all sides. Almost. The northern exposure was the most vulnerable, and it was here that most of the successful invading armies were able to penetrate the city's defenses.

I was assigned to work in Area G with Jane Cahill and David Tarler. This was the northernmost section, and highest in elevation. Kathleen Kenyon had excavated here and part of our work was to remove her dump and relocate it further down the slope. One of the problems with archaeology is that you need to make sure you don't place your dump where you may have to excavate in the future. On the other hand, thanks to the debris of ancient workers in the Valley of the Kings, the tomb of Tutankhamen was preserved until modern times.

We worked below an impressive stepped stone structure that may have been the foundation for other constructions, including the wall built by Hezekiah. The House of Ahiel was to one side, with its massive hewn ashlars to support its roof. Below this was the House of the Bullae, where fifty-one *bullae*, or seals, were discovered. A *bulla* was a baked clay seal upon which was written an inscription, e.g., "Belonging to Azaryahu son of Hilkiyahu." These date from the seventh century to early sixth century BC.

Across the "alley" from Ahiel's house was the Burnt Room. It was so named because of the carbon deposits found on the floor of the room, presumably from a fire that consumed the ceiling and supporting pillars. Here were also discovered an assortment of arrowheads, leading to speculation that this was from a period in which Jerusalem was at war, perhaps Sennacherib's invasion in 722 BC.

Just below our site was Warren's Shaft and the Gihon Spring, which marked the beginning of Hezekiah's Tunnel. This tunnel, carved out of solid rock, is a 533-meter aqueduct that empties into the Pool of Siloam. I walked through this tunnel carrying a backpack, which at times forced me to bend over in areas of low ceiling, so that my face was in the water. At certain times we just stopped, turned off our flashlights, and experienced the absolute silence and total darkness of being encased in stone. It is certainly not a place for claustrophobes.

Work on an archaeological site is more than tapping away with a handpick called a "patiche" and coming up with a magnificent find. Sometimes it can seem more like construction work. (We even used jackhammers at certain points.) Often our work entailed loading fill into wheelbarrows and taking it down the slope to dump it, and occasionally reconstructing the retaining wall below our work area so that the fill would not overflow onto the houses in the valley below.

Almost all finds are important. Shards of pottery are particularly so since they can determine the date of the stratum you are working on. The firing method and type of clay may indicate location. Design and surface writing tell clues. The different types of pottery found reveal how extensive trading had been with surrounding cultures.

Work on the site began at 7:00 a.m. and continued through the coolest part of the day. By the time we stopped, about 12:30 p.m., the temperature would be over ninety degrees. Mandatory water breaks were taken every half hour since dry heat can swiftly lead to dehydration.

There were other problems on the City of David site. The ultraorthodox Jews kept a sharp eye on the proceedings, stoning and spitting on the volunteers when they thought ancient burial places were being disturbed. Some days we worked under a police escort.

Walking to and from the City of David site could also be dangerous. One day as I was crossing the esplanade by the Western Wall, I heard the sound of gunfire. Israel police were firing their weapons as they were racing toward the Al-Aqsa Mosque on the Temple Mount. They yelled for us to lie prone, but I fumbled for my camera to get some pictures of the police action. The best I could do was to photograph the Palestinian terrorists as they were lined up to be taken away. It made sense that a sign at Christ Church Hospice would bear the words of Psalm 122:6: "Pray for the peace of Jerusalem! May they prosper who love you." The irony did not escape me. Through the centuries, Jerusalem has been one of the most violent cities, yet its name among some etymological suggestions means "City of Peace."

Each day at the site, workers would carefully wash the shards that had been soaking overnight and place them in trays to dry. Some pieces were fitted together, and a recognizable jar or jug handle would emerge. Some were deemed useless and subsequently dumped. We found it somewhat amusing that some dealers would sift through the debris to locate pieces that they would then sell in their shops to unsuspecting tourists at ridiculous prices.

Following lunch, Yigal Shiloh would conduct a briefing on the day's finds from the various areas so that all would be able to appreciate the comprehensive overview of the work. Some years later, City of David artifacts were exhibited in the United States, including Ursinus College. Hershel Shanks, founder of the Biblical Archaeology Society and longtime editor of its magazine, and I lectured at the college at the opening of the exhibit.

For the most part, the work on the City of David has been completed. The site is now open to visitors, who can explore the various areas and gain insight into biblical history almost three millennia ago.

Ein Yael

Ein Yael is an open-air museum in the Rephaim Valley outside Jerusalem, where one can learn about farming techniques and agricultural technology as was practiced nearly three thousand years ago. It is a field laboratory where research related to rural life in the biblical period can be pursued.

While today Ein Yael is a busy living museum where children and adults can experience life in biblical times, in 1985, when I took a group of volunteers to work the archaeological site, it was a remote and desolate area. Although part of the Rephaim Valley was within the municipal boundary of Jerusalem, about four miles southwest of the Old City, its steep slopes and rocky terrain deterred visitors. Even the local taxi drivers had a difficult time finding the site.

The valley is named after the race of giants that presumably inhabited the place in ancient times. It extends from the Valley of Hinnom, south of Jerusalem, and runs southwest toward Bethlehem. The Philistines were twice defeated there by David, but its primary reputation is its stony but very fertile soil, which led it to become the breadbasket of Jerusalem (cf. Isaiah 17:5).

Three sites have been worked in the valley. Khirbet Er-Ras dates from the First Temple Period (c. 1000 BC) and contains a typical four-room Palestinian house, terraces, and agricultural installations such as wine and oil presses, reservoirs, cisterns, artificially cut caves, and pathways that make it a preplanned farming unit.

Ein Yael, which gives its name to the entire site, is specifically a Roman-Byzantine location. It contains a spring (*ein* in Hebrew), a Roman bath, and the remains of a Byzantine church.

The third area is the Canaanite site where our group excavated two rooms of a Middle Bronze II Period home (c. 1800 BCE). Several buildings have been uncovered on this slope, indicating that the area had been continually occupied with a good-size settlement.

A visitor to the valley today can still see the remains of ancient terraces, which had been constructed by the settlers whose homes we were now excavating. These agricultural terraces are still in use today, producing such crops as almonds, figs, olives, grapes, and grains.

The topography of the valley is naturally stepped, resulting from the different erosion in the soft and hard bedrock. On the front edge of the natural limestone terrace, a stone retaining wall was constructed. Inside the wall, the area was carefully built up from different materials, alternating layers of gravel, soil, and stones. Gradually, on top of this porous bed, silt and organic material accumulated to create a thin layer of topsoil.

This type of agricultural construction served two main purposes. It minimized erosion caused by the heavy winter rains, and it conserved and made maximum use of the rainwater. As the water was absorbed by the porous soil-gravel bed, surplus water flowed slowly over the bedrock to the terrace below. It is estimated that 60 percent of the hills west of Jerusalem are now covered with these terraces, most of them more than three thousand years old.

While we were excavating Canaanite farmhouses, there was located nearby a later Iron Age I installation (1200–586 BC). We saw here the remains of a wine-making process. A square treading area had been cut into the rock to prevent the grape juice from splashing out. The juice would then pour into a bell-shaped vat carved from the rock. A filtering basin between the area and the vat collected the skins, pits, and pulp.

In the wall in back of the treading area was a rectangular niche that once held a wood beam, which, when weighed down with stones, formed a primitive wine press. Here grape pulp was crushed to give additional flavor to the wine.

At the City of David excavations, we had found pottery handles with the five-pointed star of Jerusalem. Here in the Rephaim were found two jar handles with a seal impression on them bearing words meaning "to the king."

Some archaeologists suggest that these seals were from an early form of the International Bureau of Weights and Measures, guaranteeing accurate measurement of the vessel and quality of the wine. Others suggest that it was a form of taxation, the king's agents collecting those containers bearing the king's seal. It seems that the more we learn about the past, the more we find that things haven't changed that much after all.

At 7:30 a.m. it is still cool in Jerusalem, and the descent into the valley of Rephaim gives little hint of the 90-degree heat that will follow. The climb back up the steep slope at the end of the day will require even greater effort. One learns to appreciate the extremes of temperature in Israel, where even midsummer nights can be a cool 60 degrees, but a hot desert sun can send the thermometer soaring to 128 degrees, as it did on Mt. Masada the day we visited the ancient ruins of Herod's palace.

However, we were prepared. Head coverings were mandatory and our backpacks contained canteens and bottled water. Common problems for the unwary visitor to the Judean wilderness are heat stroke and dehydration. With virtually no humidity, an inexperienced worker is not aware of the loss of body fluids in the arid climate. It is important to drink water frequently whether one feels thirsty or not.

The first stop on our descent to the excavation site was the supply tent, really a makeshift lean-to covering a hole in the ground where the Arab caretaker stored the tools overnight. We needed pickaxes, back-shovels, buckets, goufas (rubber containers for dirt removal), brushes, trowels, and patiches (small handpicks), We also needed to carry additional water down to the site from the spring at Ein Yael.

A group of young volunteers from Germany had been excavating a Middle Bronze Age Canaanite home that was nearly four thousand years old. Some of us tried out our Pennsylvania German and high school German on our new coworkers, but we soon found that their English was much better than our German. While Israel is trilingual (Hebrew, Arabic, and English), English was the language of the dig for all volunteers.

Our assignment was to define the outer walls of the Canaanite house. The German group had cleared two rooms and found much pottery and some interesting circular depressions in the stone floor. These indentations were common and conjecture was that they were used to keep jars with rounded bottoms from tipping over. Most of the concentrated pottery finds were within the structure. Here also were some votive pieces that had been used in a ritual center within the home.

We also became familiar with Sir Leonard Woolley's law of archaeology, which says that no matter where you put your dump, you will have to dig there next. However, removing the detritus around the walls was not that difficult and soon we had a third room to the Canaanite house.

Break time came at midmorning. For those willing to make the climb to the shelters, a cup of hot Turkish coffee was waiting—a variation on the adage that if you can't beat the heat, join it. After the first day, our group decided to remain at the site. There was one tree—you might call it a large shrub—to give us shade. With sheets borrowed from the hotel we had a makeshift pavilion.

At precisely 10:30, a steam locomotive would come through the valley, pulling its antique passenger cars to Tel Aviv. Dating back to the time of the Turkish occupation of Palestine before World War I, it was another reminder that we were in the land of antiquities. And yet the tracks themselves were the dividing line between Israel and Jordan before 1967. Even in the midst of ancient dwellings we saw the realities of rapid twentieth-century transitions.

At first it appeared to be just another shard, a large fragment of an earthen jar. As four millennia of dust was brushed aside, we could see clearly that it was a skull. Gently, expert hands took over from the volunteer, and the cranial features took shape. It was definitely human skeletal remains.

A major find at an excavation site will bring the entire dig to a halt as workers from the various areas gather around to watch and speculate. The unearthing of a skull at Ein Yael was cause for high excitement, for this was the first human remains to be found on the site. Burial caves had been located earlier, farther up the slope and away from the settlement, but this discovery was made outside the walls of a Middle Bronze house, certainly not a place for normal burial.

We had on our hands a great mystery. Who was this person? How did he or she come to be buried on this spot? Was the death the result of an accident, such as a rock slide, or an invading army passing through the valley, or was it an ancient homicide? The answer may never be known.

The skull was covered again to await the expert hands of a young anthropologist from Hebrew University. A few days later we watched her go to work. The facial features became more apparent. With the skill of a dental hygienist, the teeth were picked clean, and eventually a section of vertebrae was revealed. Unfortunately, this was the extent of the human remains that were found.

The discovery of organic material is important in an archaeological excavation. Carbon-14 dating can only be used on once-living material, but this wasn't necessary since we knew by the pottery that we were in the Canaanite period, before the Hebrews arrived from Egypt. We had found other bones of animals, such as sheep and pigs. Animal bones reveal much about lifestyles and of course help substantiate the time period. Pork bones would not have been common in an Israelite settlement.

We soon learned that the skull belonged to a young girl in her late teens. This was no doubt determined by the development of her teeth. Chemical analysis of human bone can tell us much about a civilization even after four thousand years. We can learn of what their diet consisted, from what diseases they suffered, what their environment was like, and in some cases the cause of death.

Why this girl was interred outside a dwelling, close to the door, is a mystery. It must not have been intentional. In ancient times, burial was absolutely essential, whether for sanitary reasons or simply to keep a ghost from hanging around. Hebrew law demanded immediate burial, even for criminals, whose bodies were exposed to the elements longer than most. Interments in Palestine were made in caves, rock-hewn tombs, vertical shafts, and, in the Early Bronze Age, ceramic containers that look like modern cat carriers.

My own speculations are that the girl may have been the victim of an accidental death, such as a rock slide, her other bones being removed by carnivorous animals. She may have been the victim of foul play in a later age, her body being buried unwittingly in the Middle Bronze II level. She may have been killed by a marauding army. Sometimes an archaeological excavation raises more questions than it answers.

Gershon Edelstein of the Rockefeller Museum was the excavation director. He had a dream that the Rephaim Valley would once again flourish. He had hoped to see its terraces rebuilt and the intricate irrigation system reestablished so that the valley would become a field laboratory. While Gershon's dream has been partially fulfilled, modern "progress" is rapidly obscuring the record of antiquity.

The record of antiquity was all about us. A few of us were walking with Gershon through the valley. Strewn all over were shards of pottery, fragments of broken clay pots fashioned centuries ago. One member of the group picked up a shard that had an intricate design painted on it. Gershon pointed out that, regardless of their antiquity, they were totally useless, because they could not be identified with a particular archaeological site, and therefore could not be used for dating, nor could they convey any information about the potter or their original owner. It was the silent residue of the past, the detritus of a vanished civilization, like fragments of glory consigned to the scrapheap of history.

The real question is not only what we can learn from the past, but what our civilization will leave to posterity that they might learn from us.

The Sound of Emptiness

Our midmorning break at the archaeological dig in the Rephaim Valley, just outside of Jerusalem, came at 8:30. We could only work until noon since the heat would begin to climb to over one hundred degrees. I would welcome that break because it would give me a few moments to go apart from my small group of excavators and just sit and listen to the silence of the valley.

It was a silence that came not so much from the desolation of the place and the feeling of emptiness and solitude, but from my inner feeling, a need to listen and be aware of the presence of God.

There are other places where I have also experienced this sound of emptiness—early dawn on top of Masada; along the shores of the Dead Sea; in the caves of the Cappadocian hermits in Turkey, where the wind plays tricks upon the mind; inside the Great Pyramid of Cheops in Egypt, where the sense of isolation and entombment amplifies the resonance of the massive amount of stone that surrounds you.

There are empty spaces in one's life that one needs to be aware of and savor, because it is the void that gives meaning to our existence; it is the valleys that define the mountains; the spaces between the notes that contribute to the harmony of all life.

Jesus recognized this. There are many times when the Scriptures say that Jesus drew apart from the crowd to a deserted place in order to pray. Certainly, his sojourn in the wilderness became a transforming moment of his life, when he was able to clarify his goals and his mission and put things in perspective. We all need those times of emptiness that are devoid of distractions and the demands of living.

In his Sermon on the Mount, Jesus began by saying, "Blessed are you who are poor, for yours is the kingdom of God. Blessed are you who are hungry now, for you will be filled" (Luke 6:20–21). What Jesus was saying is so obvious that we often miss its meaning. You cannot fill a bowl unless it is empty. Only those who are poor, who recognize the poverty of their existence, who are not bound by the material things of earth, can ascend to the realm of the spirit. Those who dine at the tables of this life and have been satisfied by the pleasures of the flesh feel no need for spiritual fulfillment. But those who are aware of their spiritual hunger will be able to seek that which fulfills it.

It is said that nature abhors a vacuum. So does the Western mind. We don't like emptiness; we don't like silence. We want to fill it with activity, with words. The moment our kids walk in the door and stop the music on their smartphones, they turn on the television—not that they have any intention of watching it, but just so that the air is continually filled with sound. They can't understand how Abraham Lincoln could study by firelight when they must have the glow of a television screen and the mindless jabber of sitcoms to do their homework. I am sorry *Seinfeld* went off the air. Here was a Zen Buddhist program if there ever was one. It was about absolutely nothing, and if you were really aware of what was happening while you were watching it, you at least became aware of the meaninglessness of your life. We are so desperate to fill our lives with something that we really don't care what it is.

People think of meditation as some sort of activity. "Don't just do something; sit there," they would joke. But meditating is not just sitting there. It is being aware of the timelessness of the moment.[1] The apostle Paul talked about dying to the Lord so that we might live (Romans 14:8). Meditation is something like imagining yourself dead.

A Gahan Wilson cartoon has two Zen monks in robes and shaved heads, one young, one old, sitting side by side, cross-legged on the floor. The younger one is looking somewhat puzzled. The older one tells him, "Nothing happens next. This is it."[2]

When we undertake something, we want to see results. We want some consequence to our actions, even if it is only a pleasant feeling or an understanding. We can look at a work of art, but if we don't "understand" it, we shrug our shoulders and move on from it without any appreciation of it.

---

1. Kabat-Zinn, *Wherever You Go, There You Are*, 11.
2. Kabat-Zinn, *Wherever You Go, There You Are*, 14.

Meditation is different. We don't try to get anywhere in meditation, but to realize where we are. Meditation is not so much *doing* as it is *being*. People meditate because they want to relax, or experience a special state, or become a better person, or reduce some stress or pain, or break out of old habits and patterns, or become enlightened. But if you expect those things to happen, you may be disappointed. It is when you meditate without the anxiety of expecting anything from it that you will find it.

This is why God comes to us in the moments of our greatest despair. When we feel most forsaken of God, when we sense the absence of God, and feel the gnawing pangs of loneliness, God comes to us. In the hours of the deepest night when we are truly lost and can feel nothing else, then we can become aware of the presence of God.

Once a year at my church in Kutztown—and I wish that it had been more often—we experienced the resonating sounds of Tibetan and Japanese prayer bowls to help us to deeper levels of prayer and meditation. My instructions to the congregation were: do not ask what it means; do not intellectualize the experience; do not expect or anticipate any feelings or physical changes. Simply empty yourself of all distraction and let God be present to you. Be aware of your need for God and you shall be filled.

Yes, in our busy, cacaphonic lives, we need to take time to listen to the sound of silence.

Holy Ground

Exodus 3:5

Holy places are those locales where a person becomes aware of the presence of the Divine. They can also be places that are sacred to the individual, that have special significance in the formation of one's thoughts and future development. Holy places may also be sites of historical significance to a community or a nation.

Geography has been important to all the world's religions. For all Christians, it may be the Holy Sepulcher in Jerusalem and other sites associated with Jesus of Nazareth; for Jews, the Western or Wailing Wall; for Muslims, Mecca, to which a pilgrimage must be made in the course of one's lifetime. Roman Catholics would regard Lourdes, Fatima, and Rome among sites where the miraculous is believed to have occurred.

Celtic places of special significance would be Iona, Glendalough, Lindisfarne, Glastonbury, and Croagh Patrick. Ancient Greeks would journey to Delphi, Mt. Olympus, or Parnassus to seek the wisdom of the gods.

Among the Eastern religions, Hindus have Badrinath, Puri, Dwarkha, and Rameshwaram; and Buddhists regard Buddha's birthplace at Lumbini, Nepal and the Mahabodhi Temple, site of the Bodhi Tree, under which Gautama Siddhartha found enlightenment.

While I have visited many of the sites in Israel and Europe, and some in the United States, the sense of holiness has often eluded me, greatly diminished by noisy tourists, merchants of trivial souvenirs, and the over-commercialization of religion. I have understood clearly why Jesus overturned the tables of the moneylenders at the temple.

In most cases in the Old Testament, a place was considered holy because of one person's encounter with God. When Jacob was at Beth El, he had a dream: "Then Jacob woke from his sleep and said, 'Surely the LORD is in this place—and I did not know it!' And he was afraid, and said, 'How awesome is this place! This is none other than the house of God, and this is the gate of heaven'" (Genesis 28:16).

Moses on Mt. Horeb heard the voice of God speaking from the burning bush, "Take off your sandals, for the place where you are standing is holy ground" (Exodus 3:5). It is not that God isn't elsewhere, but the holy place is where the God within us becomes more apparent. Discalced Carmelite friars are "without shoes" because they live in the presence of the Divine. Holy ground is wherever one is made aware of the indwelling spirit; and as St. Paul said that we should "pray without ceasing," so must we live in the constant awareness of "God with us"—Immanuel.

The ancient Hebrews believed that God rested in the ark of the covenant, which carried the tablets of law given to Moses. God was revealed through the law, God's words given to the people. It was a means of objectifying the inspiration and enlightenment given to Moses. (We might compare this to Siddhartha's enlightenment under the Bodhi Tree.)

When the Hebrews ceased being a nomadic people, they created a permanent dwelling for God in the temple that was erected by Solomon in Jerusalem. The ark of the covenant rested in the central part of the temple, the holy of holies, where no one was allowed to enter, except the high priest, and he only on the Day of Atonement. Even today, Orthodox Jews will not go on the Temple Mount for fear of stepping into the place where the holy of holies is believed to have been located. I worked on an archaeological project just below the Temple Mount and the Western Wall and witnessed the religious significance that this site has for Jews and Muslims.

The Western Wall was a retaining wall for the Temple Mount area on which Herod built the second temple, which the Romans destroyed in 70 AD. Since it is all that remains from ancient times, it became a place of mourning for the Jews and was also called the Wailing Wall. It is known to Muslims as al-Buraq, where the Prophet's winged horse, Buraq, was tethered. Mohammad is believed to have ascended into heaven from just above the wall, now the site of the Dome of the Rock, where Jews believe God created the world.

On my way to the City of David archaeological project, I would walk each day through the Old City, across the Western Wall Plaza, and through

Dung Gate. Often I would pause to watch those praying at the wall. One day I noticed a particularly fervent young Orthodox Jew davening at the wall. Davening is prayer often accompanied by nodding the head and rocking the body. The young man was so engaged that he was banging his head against the wall to the point that his face was bloodied. Attendants had to come and remove him. Such religious zeal can lead to an altered state of consciousness, and can be dangerous.

Two sites of special significance for me in Israel were the stillness on the Mount of Beatitudes in Galilee and the eerie silence of a morning sunrise on Masada. It reminded me of Elijah on Mount Horeb, where God said to the prophet:

> "Go out and stand on the mountain before the Lord, for the Lord is about to pass by.' Now there was a great wind, so strong that it was splitting mountains and breaking rocks in pieces before the Lord, but the Lord was not in the wind; and after the wind an earthquake, but the Lord was not in the earthquake; and after the earthquake a fire, but the Lord was not in the fire; and after the fire a sound of sheer silence." (1 Kings 19:11–12)

When there are no distractions, either from the natural world or from the noise of human interaction, when one is alone with the silence of one's own thoughts, one can hear the voice of God speaking in the language of one's own mind.

For centuries, humans have used chemicals of their own making to achieve union with the Divine. Sometimes they can be natural, and therefore the places where they were found would be considered sacred. Delphi was sacred to the Greeks because of the oracle in which the Pythia, priestess of Apollo, would sit on a tripod over a rock from which noxious hallucinogenic vapors would induce a trance-like state in which she would communicate with the Divine. From this altered state of consciousness she would pronounce the fate of the seeker.

Likewise, there are places that have been revered by Native Americans. The Hopi, Navajo, and Pueblo have sacred places in the Southwest that have psychoactive properties. The use of peyote in healing ceremonies and religious practices was common among many indigenous tribes. Many sites were regarded as sacred to Native Americans. One Navajo was once asked where these holy places could be found; his answer was all around you, for the earth itself is sacred. (More on this as we discuss creation spirituality.)

In Celtic tradition, which emphasized panentheism—the presence of God in all things—the earth, as the creation of God, was also considered the dwelling place of God. This tradition recognized that the environment has an effect upon the development of the fetus in the womb. It is not unusual for a person in Ireland to ask upon greeting a stranger, "Where are you from?" One's relationship to place and family is regarded as important, and demonstrates the connections we have with one another.

I have a friend who practices the art of dowsing. This is one of those pseudoscientific superstitions that the German immigrants brought over from the old country, whereby the dowser, using a forked branch, is able to locate water, buried metal, or even a grave. There is no science behind this, but I have often wondered if the dowser is able to detect subtle variations in a geomagnetic field. Birds, dolphins, and other animals have a physiological capacity to detect these variations, and many have a homing instinct that enables them to return to a particular place that is familiar to them. Is it also possible that humans, as well as discarnate spirits, desire to return to a place they call home?

Mystical experiences can be induced by places with weak electromagnetic fields that help us encounter a larger dimension of being or the collective unconscious that Carl Jung wrote about.

Places become infused with our presence and energy. In my study of the paranormal, particularly hauntings, I noted that ghosts don't travel, but are usually associated with places that hold meaning for them. The hitchhiking ghost stories are of entities that constantly seek to return home.

My mother lived in the house where she was born, a small house that was known in the development as "two-up, two-down." She had enough resources to live anywhere she wanted and owned a condo in Puerto Rico, but her choice was the Ironbound section of Newark, New Jersey. Whenever she was away, she always spoke of returning to her "sacred space."

There is always a desire to return to our special place. In the Scottish folk song "Loch Lomond," a dying Jacobite soldier wrote:

> Oh, ye'll tak the high road, and I'll tak the low road,
> And I'll be in Scotland afore ye;
> But me and my true love will never meet again
> On the bonnie, bonnie banks o' Loch Lomond.

The "low road" may be a reference to the Celtic belief that if someone dies away from his homeland, his soul will return home. The soldier awaiting death may have been writing either to a friend who was allowed to live and return home or to a lover back in Scotland.

Many writers would go to a special place to encounter their muse and find inspiration for their work. Ernest Hemingway, a favorite author of mine, for example, had several places of special significance for him. He spent much time in Paris with his "lost generation" associates, but he also frequented places in Italy, Spain, Cuba, Key West, and the Caribbean. Each location had its own unique activity and associations that inspired Hemingway's writings. He drew from the power of place.

The holiness of a particular place can be of short duration, or even momentary. I experienced holy ground with friends at Mensch Mill, Pennsylvania, walking the labyrinth in Chartres Cathedral, listening to the chanting of Benedictine monks in an English cathedral, walking through Gethsemane and the Via Dolorosa in Jerusalem, having espresso with my brother and uncle in the Piazza Navona in Florence. It is not just the place, but what one brings to it that makes it holy, for holy ground is always under your feet when you are aware of the presence of God.

I visited the Isle of Mull, off the western coast of Scotland, and was very much impressed with the laid-back attitude of the residents when you get away from the tourist sites. I commented on the easygoing nature of the people and tranquil environment of the island. A Mull native agreed and said that recently a Spanish tourist had asked him if they have such a word as "*manana*," meaning "tomorrow," used often for procrastination. "No," the native replied, "I don't think we have any word indicating that degree of urgency."

It would do us well to take the time wherever we are just to appreciate the place, be aware for the meaning it has for us, and contemplate the presence of God in our heart and mind.

GOD IN THE HIGH PLACES

Mountains in many religions are special places for the Divine-human encounter. The Gospels tell us that Jesus of Nazareth took Peter, James, and John and led them up a high mountain where they were alone. Luke says they went up to pray, but what began with prayer turned into an intense religious experience, the exact nature of which is uncertain. Matthew says they saw a vision. Whatever it was, it was unnatural and very mystical.

Throughout the Bible, almost all of the truly important events affecting God's relationship to his people occurred on mountaintops. To the psalmist of the Old Testament, who lived in harmony with his natural environment, the mountains represented strength and power. To primitive humans, mountains were fearful places, the dwelling place of powerful spirits; they were to be avoided if possible. The Greeks believed that the home of all the gods was on Mount Olympus. When Moses tended Jethro's herds in the land of Midian, he was told that the Lord God Yahweh lived on Mount Horeb. It was here that Moses first encountered God in the burning bush. It is no wonder that the psalmist looked to the hills for his help.

From the very beginning, mountains figure prominently in the Bible. Mount Ararat is the mountain of deliverance upon which the ark finally rested and God delivered Noah and his family from a watery grave. It was from this mount that Noah saw the rainbow sign of hope that God would save him and his descendants.

Mount Sinai is the mountain of law upon which God gave to Moses the commandments by which his chosen people were to live, and it was upon Mount Nebo that Moses saw the fulfillment of God's promise. Standing alone on the summit of Nebo—alone, except for the companionship and call of God, whom he had never forsaken—Moses looked into the promised land across the Jordan, which he was not allowed to enter.

As his people crossed the river, Moses saw the realization of his generation's striving, the accomplishment of an agony of effort, the fulfillment of their dreams for freedom. Here on Pisgah's lofty peak Moses died, and the scripture says "his sight was unimpaired and his vigor had not abated" (Deuteronomy 34:7), for though he knew he could not possess the promised land, he would meet his Lord and fulfill his ultimate dream.

It was on Mount Zion that Solomon built the temple, and this holy hill became the mountain of worship for all Jews. Mount Carmel is the mountain of decision, where the prophet Elijah commanded the people to choose between God and Ba'al. It was on Carmel that the contest between Elijah and the priests of Ba'al was held, when the fire of God consumed the sacrificial bull, and the people acknowledged that the Lord is God and he alone would they serve.

All the important events in the life of Jesus occurred on mountaintops. Before he began his ministry he was led to the Mount of Temptation and shown all the kingdoms of the world and their glory. He rejected this and went down to carry out his mission of salvation.

The greatest words ever spoken to the human race came in Jesus' Sermon on the Mount. The revelation of Jesus' divine mission occurred on Mount Hermon—the Mount of Transfiguration. On the Mount of Olives Jesus suffered the torture and agony of facing his accusers and giving himself up to die. And it was on the hill of Golgotha, "the Place of the Skull," that Christ triumphed over the forces of sin and darkness.

It is understandable that many occasions of spiritual enlightenment occur on mountaintops. It is not that one is closer to the God that is perceived to dwell in the heavenly realms above the earth. More likely, one is more aware of the indwelling spirit in lonely places, aloof from the crowds and distractions on the plains or in the cities. On the mountaintop we are more aware of the God within, whose voice can more clearly be heard.

Gospel of Grass

I grew up in the New York area when the popular music of the time was giving way to rock. I had gone to the same school as Sarah Vaughn and knew her style of jazz, and I was acquainted with Connie Francis's family. (I later performed a wedding for her cousin.) But it was a kid around the corner on Lafayette Street who had his own band that played hillbilly music who introduced me to a genre that I had only known from watching Roy Rogers movies.

Jimmy Dale was a frequent guest on Don Larkin's *Hometown Frolic*, a radio show that played country-western music every Saturday morning. While I often wondered how the "Sons of the Pioneers" would take all those instruments, including a double bass, on their cattle drives, I was also curious why mountain music was so popular in the big city.

Later on I came to realize that if Jesus had a guitar, he would probably be playing country music around the campfire with his disciples. Just think about it. Jesus was not a city person. He was literally a "cow boy," born in a stable, and grew up in a small town to the north of Jerusalem. It was a rural area that was regarded by the sophisticated Jerusalemites as backward and unsophisticated, much the same way as New Yorkers would look at Appalachia and the South today.

Jesus came from hillbilly country. In biblical times, it was the North that was rough and crude. Jesus' disciples were mocked for their accent and ridiculed by the scribes and Pharisees for their lack of etiquette and disregard for the laws of cleanliness. Nevertheless, Jesus carried his message to the city and to the world.

While we may not want to adopt the lifestyle of bluegrass performers, it would help us to understand their values and the simplicity of their faith, which was not as philosophical and theological and erudite as some of our mainline churches. The characteristics of bluegrass hymns and songs are the simplicity of faith, trust in God, Bible-based beliefs, and hope in the afterlife.

Bluegrass was inspired by the music of Appalachia. Some of it derived from Irish, Scottish, Welsh, and English traditional ballads. As early settlers, and particularly Irish immigrants in the mid-nineteenth century, moved south, their music was influenced by the sounds of African Americans, which became the root of twentieth-century jazz. While much of the music has its origins in folk tunes, there is a subgenre of bluegrass gospel, where Christian lyrics and soulful three- or four-part harmony are featured.

Gospel music grew out of America's heartland and influenced other forms of music that have been identified with the national culture. The religious identity of Americans can be said to have its basis in the rural revivals of the early nineteenth century and the emergence of evangelicalism. Gospel music not only solidified the tenets of the Judeo-Christian heritage and its values, but also helped shape the culture through which the collective hopes, dreams, and beliefs of most Americans found expression.

Many of the songs and hymns that are sung in some churches today do not necessarily reflect modern theological interpretation. They are meant to appeal to the emotions. A recent discussion among some colleagues about the theology of "The Old Rugged Cross" or the sexual mysticism of "In the Garden" pointed to the need for newer hymns, not only because of theology, but because of cultural changes that demand inclusive language.

In the film *Cool Hand Luke*, Paul Newman sings "Plastic Jesus," which two high school kids, Ed Rush and George Cromarty, had written a decade before after hearing a radio program pitching religious trinkets.

While there is humor in much of bluegrass gospel music, many of the lyrics distort the real message of Christianity and appeal to other parts of human nature. Some people want a religion that appeals to the heart and not to the brain. All too often religion is judged solely on the basis of how it makes a person feel. There is nothing wrong with this. Music should emanate from within the soul.

Bluegrass music reflects the hard life and poverty of the rural South, of mountainfolk trying to eke out an existence and having nothing to look forward to except the next life. One of the popular songs of the nineteenth century was "Poor Wayfaring Stranger," which grafted African American spiritual lyrics onto an Irish tune and speaks to the age-old themes of loss and reunion in the next world.

> I'm a poor wayfaring stranger
> While traveling thru this world of woe
> Yet there's no sickness, toil, or danger
> In that bright world to which I go
> I'm going there to see my Father
> I'm going there no more to roam
> I'm only going over Jordan
> I'm only going over home.
> I know dark clouds will hang 'round me,
> I know my way is rough and steep
> Yet beauteous fields lie just before me
> Where God's redeemed their vigils keep
> I'm going there to see my mother
> She said she'd meet me when I come
> I'm only going over Jordan
> I'm only going over home.

Bluegrass and Southern gospel and other like genres will continue to have an influence on America's music, and we can learn to appreciate their unique place in our history without necessarily subscribing to some of their theology. But at its core are solid foundations—to live in harmony with our brothers and sisters, to trust in God, and to know that there is a life in the presence of God after we are finished here.

In many of our churches there are people who listen to the lyrical content of gospel songs to test their faithfulness to Scripture and theology. They raise the question: "Do the song's lyrics reflect sound doctrine?" When it comes to bluegrass, let the music do the speaking and listen to the heart of those who perform and those who are moved by it. Sometimes it is best to lay aside preconceived notions and ideas, and let the word of God speak plainly to us. Music has a way of doing that. Listen not only with your mind, but with your heart and soul.

Our Soul's Longing

It is said that when you really want something, the desire drives you to attain it. It is the intensity of prayer on a subconscious level that brings about its fulfillment. It is the soul's longing that puts one in a position to attain that which is really the heart's desire. We relentlessly pursue that which is important to us. Unfortunately, much too often that which we desire and pursue is of little value in the grand scheme of things. The collector who spends a fortune to own an antique or a work of art or a baseball card or whatever may find that when he has spent his years acquiring things, he has emptied his soul.

I once visited a resident of a nursing home. Throughout her life, she had all she needed to live comfortably: a fine house, friends, a loving husband, the respect of all who knew her. She lacked for nothing. Now she sat in her wheelchair alone in a small room and cried. "Where did it all go?" she asked. Deep inside of her, she was asking the existential question that all of us ask when faced with the nearness and inevitability of death: "What is the point of it all?" Does death really make life meaningless?

If your goal in life is to surround yourself with material things and physical comforts, you will find that when you attain them, you really do not possess them. They possess you and keep you from achieving what you are born for.

The Norwegians have a legend that before a soul enters the body that soul it is kissed by God, and during all of its life on earth the soul retains a latent memory of that kiss and relates everything to it. It is another way of saying that all humans bear the imprint of God's creativity.

In Jewish mystical writings there is also a story that when God puts a soul into a body, an angel comes and whispers to the soul one word: "Forget." The angel presses the baby's mouth shut as a gesture that during its earthly life it is to be silent about its divine origins. The little crevice below each person's nose is the imprint of the angel's forefinger, sealing their lips—and that is why when you are trying to remember something, during your ponderings your own forefinger spontaneously rises and is placed in that crevice.

There is in each person a desire, a holy longing, for that which is beyond oneself, and beyond the world in which we live. Often we cannot name that feeling. It is a homing instinct to return to our Creator. The heart is restless until it finds its rest in God.

Thomas Wolfe, in the very opening of *Look Homeward, Angel*, asks, "Which of us is not forever a stranger and alone . . . lost! Remembering speechlessly we seek the great forgotten language, the lost lane-end into heaven . . . an unfound door."[1] At the deathbed of his brother Ben, Eugene Gant, the principal character, who does not believe in God, or in heaven or hell, nevertheless feels that he must pray.

> He did not believe in angels with soft faces and bright wings, but he believed in the dark spirits that hovered above the heads of lonely men . . . All that he had read in books, all the tranquil wisdom he had possessed so glibly in his philosophy courses. . . left him now, under the mastering urge of his wild Celtic superstition . . . So, with insane singsong repetition, he began to mutter over and over again: "Whoever you are, be good to Ben tonight. Show him the way."[2]

Even those who do not know God find themselves crying out to the void as though there is a God who can hear them, like Bartimaeus, without seeing, cries out for deliverance. Our soul's longing is for God, whether in the emptiness of the universe where God seems absent or in our own lives. As prodigal children, we have moved away from God, yet in the far country we remember our home and where we belong.

We are familiar with the pain of living, of dealing with difficult people, of raising children who disappoint us, of losing a job, of facing a life-ending illness, of breaking a relationship that we thought would go on forever. We deal with our share of life's tragedies.

1. Wolfe, *Look Homeward, Angel*, 1.
2. Wolfe, *Look Homeward, Angel*, 464.

But we also have those times when things just seem to come together and make sense and affirm life. Even our struggles and pains remind us that life is still wonderful and beautiful because there is more to it than we can see at any given moment. There are no accidents or coincidences, but life is moving toward a fulfillment beyond our immediate comprehension.

In 1949 a young soldier returned home from the war to find his mother desperately ill with kidney problems. She needed an immediate blood transfusion to save her life. Unfortunately, no one in the family shared the mother's very rare blood type of AB negative, and blood banks didn't exist in those days.

The young soldier decided to gather his family together to say goodbye to his mother. As he was driving home from the hospital, he stopped to pick up another young soldier who was hitchhiking. The hitchhiker noticed the young man's tears and asked him what was wrong. The young man blurted out the story of his dying mother. In silence, the hitchhiker took off his dog tags and held them out to the young man. On the tags was listed his blood type: AB negative. The mother received her transfusion that night and recovered fully. She lived another forty-seven years after that fateful night.[3]

There are no coincidences. The soldier and his family believed that it was God's intervention and that the hitchhiker was an angel sent by God. There is intentionality in the universe. When we are patient, we may see that there is reason behind the events of our lives. If the hitchhiker would not have appeared, the soldier's life would have followed another course, but there would still be reason behind it.

God promised Jeremiah that he would bring the remnant of Israel, the scattered community, together. Jesus healed the spiritual blindness of people who could not see how close they were to the kingdom of God. Within each of us God has placed a restlessness that finds no rest until it discovers God. May we be fortunate to know the work of God in our own lives and express our gratitude with generous and joyful living.

---

3. Divine Intervention, "Reflections for Sunday, October 25, 2016," at http://www.thedivineintervention.org/2016-reflections.html.

"Your Mother Is Dying"

Gabe Fackre taught a course on "Church in Society" at Lancaster Seminary. I was so motivated by his social justice emphasis that in my first church in rural Pennsylvania I sought to proclaim the gospel in terms of righting the wrongs of our culture and political system. Unfortunately, the classroom did not always translate well to the pulpit. In opposing war, I incurred the wrath of the local American Legion post, whose president was also president of my congregation. I also attempted to continue my work in race relations, but that too fell on deaf ears since most members considered equal rights irrelevant to their all-White fellowship. The church, however, had no objection to my working with ecological issues.

In 1969 there was growing awareness of impending environmental catastrophe facing our planet. After reading Rachel Carson's *Silent Spring*, about the growing use of pesticides, and Paul Ehrlich's *The Population Bomb*, predicting worldwide famine beginning in 1970, I started accumulating a small library of books on various ecological problems. Life on our planet was growing more tenuous. Indeed, Gaia, our Earth Mother, was believed to be *in extremis*, and one of the warnings of the ecological movement was that "your mother is dying," and that she was already in need of hospice care.

I joined several environmental activist groups and went to New York City to meet with David Brower, president of Friends of the Earth. His encouragement led me to become a regional organizer for the first Earth Day observance in 1970, coordinating the efforts among several colleges in the Lehigh Valley, which included Muhlenberg, Moravian, Cedar Crest, Lafayette Colleges, and Lehigh University. It also included several local eco-protection groups that gathered under the umbrella of the Lehigh Valley Environment Federation, which I initiated.

In developing this coalition, I met with a number of environmentalists and professors, including Dr. Carl Oplinger of Muhlenberg College and Dr. Francis Trembley of Lehigh University. Oplinger did a detailed environmental analysis of the Lehigh Valley and his concern for the degrading ecological system inspired me to work more fervently. Trembly was promoting Charles Darwin's "entangled bank" concept of habitat protection for wildlife species, whereby people should set aside portions of their grounds and just let them grow wild so that all forms of life might have an opportunity to grow and support one another. Trembly founded Lehigh's ecology department in 1949 and created its curriculum.

Gathering all these resources and meeting with local environmentalists also involved enlisting our local judicatory's support. As chair of the local Christian Witness Committee in the Penn Northeast Conference, I was able to convene a number of meetings in various locations to rally persons to the cause. One member of our planning group was Bob Rodale, whose father, J. I. Rodale, started an organic farming and gardening enterprise in nearby Emmaus. Bob would show up at these meetings carrying a bag of groceries and would proceed to read off the list of ingredients on the packages, pointing out how these consumables were poisoning us. Bob took over the company when his father died of a heart attack while taping *The Dick Cavett Show*. Unfortunately, Bob was killed in an auto accident in Russia, but the company continued its advocacy for a healthier, organic food supply.

A THEOLOGICAL FOUNDATION FOR CREATION SPIRITUALITY

There is a Hopi myth in which two brothers part ways to search for their father, Maasauu, a clan chief who has disappeared into darkness after tasting evil. The younger brother remains with the Hopi, while the older brother, Pahana, travels eastward with a piece of a sacred stone tablet in his possession. The tablet contains the Hopi laws for living. The myth says that Pahana will return when it is time to restore balance to the world, reuniting the missing piece to the whole.

The Hopi will recognize their lost brother, continues the myth, because he will not only have the ancient wisdom; he will have new wisdom learned through his wanderings. This reunion will occur only when Pahana remembers his original connection to the Hopi, to the inner earth wisdom that he has forgotten on his sojourns. Then, and only then, will the inner and outer unite to birth a true whole.[1]

Many years and many journeys separate us from this Hopi creation story, yet its message is a metaphor for our times. Pahana's need to remember, to rejoin his new wisdom to his ancestral knowledge, parallels the needs of our own civilization. In this twenty-first century we have been dazzled by the gifts that science and technology have showered upon us. We have learned much. But we have also forgotten much.

We have forgotten that the earth, which has given us the raw materials with which we have fashioned our lives, is a living organism. Like the human body, the ecosystems of the earth must work in harmony. The ancient wisdom taught that the earth is our mother and that we must take of her. Unfortunately, we have acted more like a destructive virus that is killing our mother, and therefore ourselves.

A statement written in the 1970s, but attributed to the Native American Chief Seattle, reflects the ancient wisdom of our ancestors:

> All things are connected like the blood which unites one family . . . Whatever befalls the earth, befalls the children of the earth. People did not weave the web of life; they are merely a strand of it. Whatever they do to the web, they do to themselves.[2]

Because of the way we, her children, have treated her, Mother Earth has aged dramatically in the last century. Her health is becoming increasingly fragile and precarious. If she dies or becomes extremely sick, adoption out to another home is not really an option.

Topsoil, species, farmland, and forests are decreasing at an alarming rate, as the human population continues to increase, placing greater demands on our mother's limited resources. When the rainforests are eliminated, we will have amputated 40 percent of our mother's lungs, which provide the oxygen we need to live. The mainstream scientific community acknowledges that ozone depletion and planetary climate change (the "greenhouse effect") are ominously already upon us and we are seeing the results of global warming in changing weather patterns and rising ocean

---

1. Boissiere, *Return of Pahana* (1990), quoted in Pion, "Ecocommunion."
2. Clinebell, *Ecotherapy*, 1.

levels. We don't have much time to reverse the treatment of Mother Earth, or the damage to her may become irreversible.

We in the church have contributed substantially to this abuse of Mother Earth. In the late 1980s a Yale University–funded study discovered that in the United States, the more a person participated in religious services, the less concern he or she would have for nature. Our theology taught us that we are to dominate and subdue the earth. We need a new theology and a creation-centered spirituality that focuses on the other Genesis story of creation—that we are to care for the earth. We need to unite the new wisdom to the old wisdom.

In the first story of creation, at the completion of each act or day of creation, we read, ". . . and God saw that it was good."

Everything in creation, living and inanimate, is good, holy, precious, blessed by God, filled with the divine radiance. Matthew Fox has stated eloquently in his books *Original Blessing* and *The Coming of the Cosmic Christ* that "traditional" theology has been preoccupied with the sin and redemption of the individual human soul and been blind to creation and creativity. By recovering our intrinsic wonder and awe at creation, we place ourselves in the living tradition of Hebrew spirituality, Jesus the nature lover, Celtic Christianity, St. Francis of Assisi, Meister Eckhart, Hildegard of Bingen, Mechteld of Magdeburg, Julian of Norwich, and Native American spirituality.

Our theology and worldview has been anthropocentric—centered on humanity. The biblical vision is generally cosmic and ecological. At the completion of the flood story, God makes a covenant, symbolized in the rainbow, with Noah and every living thing. (The sign of the covenant is used seven times just to drive the point home.) Not only human beings, but everything that has breath, is called upon to praise God (Psalms 148 and 150; Revelation 5:11). Jesus recognized that all living things are good and valuable in the eyes of God. "Are not five sparrows sold for a farthing? And not one of them is forgotten before God" (Luke 12:6). The book *When Elephants Weep* points out that animals feel with a depth as great as or greater than we humans have. "God so loved the world" means that when a species becomes extinct, God's heart is broken.[3]

The world is still in need of love—God's and ours. The old wisdom of the Bible and many of the earth's peoples calls us to love of our Mother

---

3. Borglum, "Honoring Our Mother," 1.

Earth and help her to survive. Edward O. Wilson calls it "biophilia"—a love of living things or "Earth-love."[4]

Many persons do not realize that Al Gore, who wrote *A Necessary Truth*, not only graduated with honors from Harvard University but also attended Vanderbilt University's Graduate School of Religion. His environmental concerns have been informed by a consistent psychological and spiritual awareness. In his book *Earth in the Balance*, Gore reminds us of Jesus' Parable of the Unfaithful Steward, which tells us something about the dangers of the way we treat our planet. You remember in the parable that the master goes on a journey and leaves his servant in charge of the house. He says, essentially, "While I am gone, if vandals ransack this house or steal my belongings, it will not be a good enough excuse for you to say, 'I was asleep.'"

"In our relationship with this planet, we have become like the unfaithful servant—even as we witness environmental vandalism on a global scale, we are implicitly preparing to say we were asleep. The effects of global warming, the emergence of many powerful new technologies, and our own dysfunctional attitudes toward the Earth are manifesting themselves at a rapidly increasing rate. Human civilization and the natural world are on a collision course, and the only way to change that is to wake up from our unhealthy attitudes toward the planet and find a new model" to relate to the ancient wisdom for the way we treat the Earth.[5]

Gore suggests that we revisit the ancient wisdom of our faith and reexamine the Judeo-Christian tradition. We should look again at the Old Testament story of Noah's ark and recognize that God made a covenant with Noah to preserve biodiversity, to care for and ensure the reproduction of all God's creatures.

The environmental movement that began on Earth Day in 1970 has evolved from simply predicting the dire consequences of our actions to affirming an earth spirituality in which we relate to God through a love for God's creation. A Bulgarian folk song says, "The earth is our mother. She will take care of you." But we must also take care of her. We must practice what Howard Clinebell calls "ecotherapy," the healing of ourselves through the healing of the earth.[6]

---

4. Wilson, *Biophilia*.
5. Gore, "Story of the Earth and Us."
6. Clinebell, *Ecotherapy*.

Pahana, the Hopi brother of the ancient myth, has returned, and the new wisdom is blending with the old. It may be too late for some of us to appreciate the need to love the earth, but it is not too late for our children to be sensitive to the cries of pain that emerge from our mother.

The writer of John's Gospel said that "God so loved the world that he sent his Son" (John 3:16).

Forty years ago, we sang "What the World Needs Now Is Love." The world still needs love. And it's time for all of us to fall back in love with our Mother Earth.

Thank You

A seminary education cannot prepare you for all the exigencies of life. We learn much more by our experiences and the people we encounter, especially as we share their pain and suffering.

It was only a month into my first pastorate, in rural Pennsylvania when I was called to the hospital, where a young man in his late thirties was dying. For the past twenty years, Barry had consumed barrels of beer and hard liquor and was now paying the bill. His liver was failing and the severe cirrhosis had tinted his skin a bright yellow. He could hardly speak, but he wanted the prayers of the church he had neglected, even though his parents were regular attenders and had lifted him in prayer each week.

I offered Barry as much comfort as I could and hoped I had said the right words, but he was not interested in words. He was just grateful for my presence and the congregation I was representing. His parents, and his friends, including a girl he had once loved, who could no longer deal with his alcoholism, were also in the room. When all the words that needed to be said were spoken, Barry turned toward me, smiled, and said, "Thank you." And then he died.

Many years later, when I visited Copenhagen, I heard of a village with a beautifully landscaped cemetery next to the community church. It is reported that at least a third of the gravestones there have an inscription with just three letters, "TAK," which is Danish for "Thanks." Some stones read "TAK FOR ALT," meaning "Thanks for everything." Were these the final words of the deceased expressing gratitude for life, or were these the words of loved ones thanking the departed for being a part of their lives?

Thank You

The Danes are an extremely polite people, and the expression "*Tak for alt*" is used at the time of departure, whether from a brief stay at one's home or the final departure at the end of our days.

One of the preeminent psychologists of the last century quietly passed almost unnoticed from the world stage at the age of ninety-one. Viktor Frankl had been a prisoner of the Nazis at Auschwitz during World War II, and had witnessed the worst that humanity could inflict upon itself. Dr. Gordon Allport, in his preface to Frankl's significant work *Man's Search for Meaning*, says that there "he found himself stripped to a literally naked existence. His father, mother, brother and his wife died in the camps or were sent to the gas ovens, so that except for his sister, his entire family perished in these camps. How could he—every possession lost, every value destroyed, suffering from hunger, cold and brutality, hourly expecting extermination—how could he find life worth preserving? A psychiatrist who personally has faced such extremity is a psychiatrist worth listening to."[1]

Frankl answers Allport's question when he recounts his experience immediately following his liberation from the camps:

> One day, a few days after the liberation, I walked through the country, past flowering meadows, for miles and miles, toward the market town near the camp. Larks rose to the sky and I could hear their joyous song. There was no one to be seen for miles around; there was nothing but the wide earth and sky and the larks' jubilation and the freedom of space. I stopped, looked around and up to the sky—and then I went down on my knees. At that moment there was very little I knew of myself or of the world—I had but one sentence in mind—always the same: "I called to the Lord from my narrow prison and he answered me in the freedom of space."[2]

While in the prison camp at Theresienstadt, Frankl was on a work detail one dark, gray morning, struggling to find meaning for his suffering. He looked into the distance and saw a light go on in a Bavarian farmhouse, and the words came to him: "*Et lux in tenebris lucet*"—"And the light shines in the darkness." When he emerged from the concentration camp, he fell on his knees and was able to say "thank you" for life and for hope.

The thirteenth-century German philosopher and mystic Meister Eckhart said, "If the only prayer you ever say in your entire life is 'thank you,' it will be enough."

1. Frankl, *Man's Search for Meaning*, vii–viii.
2. Frankl, *Man's Search for Meaning*, 141–42.

The deepest gratitude comes from deliverance and restoration. Dostoevsky saw doubt not as a devil, but as an angel. In *The Brothers Karamazov*, he wrote, "my hosannas have been forged in the crucible of doubt." *Hosanna* is the Hebrew word for gratitude and praise, a cry of deliverance when one has been rescued. When you are in the worst possible situation, your inner spirit returns to God and you come to terms with the One who is able to save. No matter what life may give us, we will emerge and once again behold the stars, and be grateful.

Dover Beach

We arrived early at the port of Dover, where we would embark on our voyage through the North Sea and the Baltic Sea. I had time to stand on the deck of our ship on that cloudy morning and see the famed White Cliffs of Dover, which were such a welcome sight to the returning airmen of the Second World War who made it home after their perilous bombing runs over Germany. The cliffs represented a safe return, but also a longing for peace, a hope that the war would soon end.

Nearly a century earlier, the poet Matthew Arnold stood on Dover Beach, not far from where our ship was docked. He too was impressed with the view, but he had an altogether different understanding. The sea was calm that night; there was a melancholy sadness about it, an eternal note that echoed across the centuries from the time of Sophocles, who

> Heard it on the Aegean, and it brought
> Into his mind the turbid ebb and flow
> Of human misery; we
> Find also in the sound a thought,
> Hearing it by this distant northern sea.

For Matthew Arnold, it is the Sea of Faith that tests us in times of trial and uncertainty and asks us to hold on to love as the only thing that can help us transcend the pain of this life. He concludes his poem "Dover Beach" with these lines:

> Ah, love, let us be true
> To one another! for the world, which seems
> To lie before us like a land of dreams,

> So various, so beautiful, so new,
> Hath really neither joy, nor love, nor light,
> Nor certitude, nor peace, nor help for pain;
> And we are here as on a darkling plain
> Swept with confused alarms of struggle and flight,
> Where ignorant armies clash by night.[1]

We are still on the darkling plains and ignorant armies are still clashing by night, stumbling in the dark without clear objectives. When shall we learn that love is more powerful than hate, and that the world was changed by a man who took all that his enemies could inflict on him, yet said not a word in anger, but accepted the cross? It is strange that we worship this man, but we do not emulate him. We acknowledge his teachings, but we do not follow them. By our silence we are complicit in the evils of our day.

As followers of the Christ, we need to do more than acknowledge the words of love and forgiveness. We must be the embodiment of God's love in all that we do, whether it is to persons or to nations and societies. We must work together to achieve the "land of dreams" of joy, love, light, certitude, peace, and help for the pain that is within us and within the soul of the world.

---

1. Quoted in Untermeyer, *Treasury of Great Poems*, 922.

Celtic Journeys

The divergent streams of one's life's journey eventually blend together into a meaningful whole, making sense of an entire life. It's like being handed pieces of a jigsaw puzzle one at a time. We don't know how it fits together until a life is complete and we look back and say, "So that's what it's all about."

Pat embodied the Celtic spirit and taught me what it means to be Irish, though any Irish strains in my pedigree would be minimal, or at least unknown to the members of my tribe. A DNA analysis indicated that there was some Celtic blood in our lineage. Pat couldn't quite convince me that the best part of being Irish is learning how to get drunk and enjoy it. Since I am not Irish, I always got to be the designated driver.

Pat had hoisted a few too many at a party and I had to get him home sober. Coffee didn't work. You don't want to have a wide-awake, hyperactive drunk. We drove around for a bit. I asked Pat to open the vent window to direct the flow of air at him and to take deep breaths in order to reoxygenate his blood. I didn't know that this was the prescribed method for rapid detoxification, but it seemed to make sense.

As lucidity returned, our conversation increased in coherence. I thought that if we talked, he would be less inclined to vomit on the dashboard of my freshly cleaned Oldsmobile.

"Have you ever been to the Old Country?" I asked.

"What's that?" he mumbled.

"You know, the Emerald Isle, the land of your ancestors."

"What for?" "Oh yeah," he quickly answered his own question, "they serve beer in larger glasses."

That conversation didn't go very far. What I liked about Pat and his family was that they were the stereotypical Irish American family. His father was a fireman. His mother worked in a factory—the same job she had during the war. They went to Mass at St. Aloysius Roman Catholic Church, the ethnic church for the Irish in our neighborhood. We never discussed religion.

The Catholic Mass was to this young outsider so much voodoo worship in the strange language of the ancient Romans, with priests bowing and genuflecting and moving around, ringing bells, and making the sign of the cross. To the uninitiated, the peculiar customs of another way are always strange. It is in understanding why people do the things that they do that we build bridges and make connections.

Pat helped me to appreciate the better parts of Irish culture. I could understand why it is said that on St. Patrick's Day everyone is Irish. I started to develop an interest in all things Irish, and by extension all things Scottish, especially the folklore and music. So much of our American folk tunes originated in Appalachia among the Scotch-Irish settlers. In high school, I read the novels of Sir Walter Scott and studied the long history of the Scottish resistance to English rule. I became familiar with William Wallace, Robert the Bruce, and Rob Roy MacGregor. I was even taken in by the romantic story of Flora MacDonald, who ferried Bonnie Prince Charlie "over the seas to Skye" after the disaster at Culloden. Unfortunately, reality often destroys the beauty of legend. I learned later that Flora was trying to get rid of the bonnie prince before he could bring harm to her family. How could the Scots be singing "Will Ye No Come Back Again" for this besotted, aristocratic pretender whose stupidity and arrogance made him *persona non grata* in many European courts?

I also discovered the dream-like quality of William Butler Yeats and was fascinated by his unrequited love for the beautiful Maude Gonne and his part in the Easter Rising. I was becoming a Celtophile and saw the cross-cultural connections between the War for American Independence and its roots in the Jacobite Rebellion of 1745. How many of those Culloden survivors came to the New World and carried on their fight against the tyranny of the British crown? Unfortunately, history is never tidy. Many of the Scots in the Carolinas became Tories and aligned with Tarleton and Cornwallis against the Americans.

While my decision to enter the Christian ministry had followed a different strand, the Celtic cord kept weaving its way back into my life's tapestry. I withdrew my application to Princeton and entered Ursinus College, a small liberal arts college in Pennsylvania established in the German Reformed tradition by the pietist John Bomberger in resistance to the radical and Romish teachings of the seminary in Lancaster. Fortunately, Ursinus had become so secularized that Bomberger's theology was negligible in the school's philosophy. While you could take a course in the history of the Pennsylvania Germans, you could also study Anglo-Saxon, one of very few American colleges at the time to require that language of its English majors.

Upon graduating Ursinus, I went over to the enemy. On my first visit to Lancaster Theological Seminary I was greeted by a sign that apparently some student had altered. It read "Lancaster the Logical Seminary." Perhaps it was a favorable sign and a logical decision, although the annual prank at Ursinus was to remove the first and last two letters over the main gateway so that prospective students would be welcomed to "Sin College."

The incoming class at Lancaster was required to spend some time in what the school called "cross-cultural studies." I was in the second class to engage in this semester abroad. The first class went to Germany, but ours went to Scotland, England, and France. It was not only a time to study the Reformed theology of the Presbyterians in Scotland, Congregationalists in England, and Huguenots in France, but also a time to be exposed to different ways of thinking and approaching life. It was in Scotland that the door opened to Celtic philosophy and appreciation for the doctrine of panentheism, seeing the spirit of God in all things. God's presence in the natural world was evident in my early youth at church camp, museum visits, and close friendships with those who contributed to my enlightenment, but visiting Scotland and later Ireland deepened my appreciation for this element of Celtic spirituality. Time spent at Iona, Glendalough, and the ceilis at a pub in Galway, meeting with John Philip Newell and reading John O'Donohue, and gathering an extensive library of books and worship resources has further enhanced the Celtic expression in my life.

I have endeavored to bring this appreciation to the people of the churches I have served by having regular Celtic worship services, using the liturgies from Iona, and having ceili bands accompany our singing. And to think that it all began in childhood from a friendship with an Irish neighbor.

Anamchara

When the terrorists flew their planes into the World Trade Center on September 11, 2001, nearly three thousand people lost their lives. Most were employees of companies with offices in the building, coming to work as on any other day. Each person had his or her reason for being there on that fateful day. There were others, for one reason or another, who decided not to be present, whether it was a premonition, or some sort of cosmic intervention, or just a coincidental alteration of plans. Why were some fated to perish and others to survive?

A woman was murdered in Philadelphia while jogging early in the morning. One of the reactions to the crime: she shouldn't have been running so early in that section. Somehow it became the victim's fault for being in the wrong place at the wrong time.

Pontius Pilate had his Romans murder some Galileans while they worshiped on Mount Gerizim and mixed their blood with those of their sacrifices. In another incident, a tower fell in the Siloam section of Jerusalem and eighteen were killed. Jesus' disciples put this question to him: Did they deserve to die because of what they did?

No, said Jesus, these are the tragedies of life. This is not the way God operates. God may have set the universe in motion, created human life, and determined a pattern for human existence. God may be concerned about how life is played out and may know what the final outcome will be. God may even respond to our pleas to change our particular situations. But within the ultimate scheme of things, it is we who determine our own destinies.

We are so ready to rush to judgment on things. We want immediate results, instant answers. We want to affix blame and guilt immediately. We want instant gratification. We have lost our sense of patience with things and with people.

The prophet Isaiah said that God has thoughts and ways that differ from our thinking and acting, because God can see the larger picture. God's perspective on our lives is put in the larger context of human history and the purpose for the cosmos. If we cannot know what that is, we must trust that God does.

A few years ago, I stood in the cemetery at Gallipoli in Turkey. It was here during World War I that young Turkish soldiers on one side and the young Australian soldiers on the other were both innocent victims of cruel and imperialist policies of the major superpowers of the time. The Australians fought for a declining British Empire and the Turks for a collapsing Ottoman Empire, which would soon cease to exist. The cemetery at Gallipoli is a sad and lonely place because it is a monument to futility. Perhaps that is why the words of the founder of modern Turkey, Kemal Ataturk, inscribed in stone on a memorial at Gallipoli, are so poignant: "You, the mothers, who sent your sons from far away countries, wipe away your tears; your sons are now lying in our bosom and are in peace. After having lost their lives on this land they have become our sons as well."

Ataturk was embracing former enemies who lost their lives on a battlefield in his country, thus becoming one with the human struggle.

If we cannot understand one another, how can we hope to understand God? We make no effort to understand Arabic culture or the Middle Eastern mindset or what the Japanese value or why the Russians are so frustrated. We do not try to understand why Black Lives Matter. We isolate ourselves from each other, and in many ways we insulate ourselves as well.

Our culture says that it is much easier to shun a problem than to deal with it. Instead of going to our relatives and friends when misunderstandings arise and seeking resolution and reconciliation, we are more inclined not to speak to them again.

I was sitting in a funeral director's office one time when he got a phone call from the daughter of a woman whose viewing was to be held that evening. She wanted to know when she could come and pay her respects to her mother; she didn't want to confront her brother, with whom she had not spoken in sixteen years.

God's ways are not our ways. God seeks reconciliation with us. God does not want us to be separated from his love. Nor does God want us to be separated from each other, because God's spirit is in each one of us. When we are separated from each other, we are fragmented and resisting God's intention for wholeness in the human family. We are breaking the wholeness of the body of Christ.

One particularly meaningful model of this unity is that of spiritual friendship. It comes from the Celtic notion of *anamchara*, or "spiritual friend." An anamchara is a friend who accompanies you on your spiritual journey. It is a person to whom you can go, who will point out to you in a loving way the pitfalls you might miss, who will encourage you in times of despair and depression, who will be with you in your times of need. An anamchara takes responsibility for you.

In the culture of the Druids, the anamchara was the spiritual advisor to kings and chieftains. With the arrival of Christianity, the anamchara became the soul friend. It was a role not just for priests and monks, although they did take on this role, but for lay men and women.

The anamchara is one who weaves the qualities of belonging, compassion, and understanding into the mysteries and possibilities of the spiritual life. It is the person who can discern the thoughts and point out the ways of God to another. The anamchara is one who can hold both her relationship with God and her relationship with her friend as sacred mirrors of each other. Since all human love flows from God, so all relationships and friendships draw their sustenance from the well of divine life.

Beyond the gifts of companionship and intimacy, the soul friend provides a reality check as we explore life, and helps us get beyond our culture's insistence upon immediate results. The soul friend helps us to see that God is not only interested in us, but in our relationships. The anamchara in ancient times was spiritually rooted in the mystical tradition of helping persons seek God through prayer and meditation. The role of an anamchara today is simply being present in times of need and helping his or her soul friend discern the thoughts and ways of God in one's life.

Who we are to each other is important. One of the strong marks of Celtic Christianity is that the natural order ordained by God necessitates that each member of the community support one another. Our strength comes from the presence of God in the life of the community, and in the recognition that every act—even mundane, everyday tasks—can express the sacred. Whether we call it the "practice of the presence of God" or the "mysticism of ordinary experience" or the "anamchara relationship," it derives from Celtic spirituality and should have a place in our own experience. We need to recognize the validity of other spiritual traditions to discern the thoughts and the ways of God, so that in the end we are all soul friends of each other.

"What Is Truth?"

There are certain fragments of memory that we retain from childhood, images that are somehow impressed in the cortex of our brains. We may not remember the context or the reason, but they stay with us for many years.

Among the cinematic fragments that lie half-buried in my memory is from a movie that I saw as a young child. The title is long forgotten and the plot of the film never registered, but the image is there. A little girl sits in an empty church for a Sunday morning worship service. The old preacher, perhaps her grandfather, preaches to the vacant pews. Rejected by his congregation, he has turned to alcohol, and yet in his drunken state the word of the Lord is proclaimed.

I have often wondered how many times truth is rejected because of the messenger. Does one spurn a gift because the packaging is unattractive? Does one dying of thirst refuse a glass of water that is not served in a crystal goblet?

The politics of the year 2020 and following, as well as many times in the past, has had many distortions of truth. What we believe to be true is often based on who is speaking. Pontius Pilate may have been correct in his question, "What is truth?"

Truth is what truth is—it stands alone apart from its container. The reverse is also true. Because the container is attractive doesn't mean that its contents are good for you.

We often look to the leader of our country to tell us the truth. Yes, there are times when deception may be necessary to accomplish a greater good. Certainly we know that in wartime or in times of national crisis lies are told to deceive an enemy or to protect the country. However, hypocrisy that is ingrained and serves no purpose reflects on the character of the person. A president who doesn't go to church professes to be a Christian and is endorsed by fundamentalist Christians, who attends a prayer breakfast where he doesn't pray but castigates his political opponents with vile language that Jesus would never use, cannot be viewed as an example of what he claims to be. We do not know what truth is anymore.

One day, a young man gave in to his compulsion to seek Truth. He traveled the world; he followed leads and legends; he made assumptions; he made mistakes; he narrowed his focus; he lost his former self in the search process; he matured; he aged. Finally, high in a remote mountain area, he met a wizened, crumbled, deceptively ugly old hag. "Tell me, Madame, what is your name?," he asked. "I am Truth," she answered, "and I am the object of your search."

The now older man spent many years with the visually offensive woman. He learned from Truth. She became his teacher, his mentor, his grandmother, his knowledge giver, his Source. He reveled in her wisdom, in her experience, in her vision. Finally, he felt that the time had come for him to go and tell of her throughout the world. "Truth," he said, "you have shared so much with me; you have been so selfless. What can I tell the world about you?," he asked.

"Tell them I am beautiful," she replied.

Truth is a lie. Truth is relative. Truth is a matter of perspective. Truth is not absolute, but changes with the context, and is subject to interpretation and the understanding of the perceiver. Juries are often hung because they cannot agree on the veracity of those who testify. Truth, the whole truth, and nothing but the truth is often shaded and distorted.

Do we ever know the whole person? The hag may have a beautiful soul. In her own eyes she may think herself beautiful. There may be parts of a person that truly are beautiful. As one jurist commented, "Truth is not only blind, but deaf, dumb, and has a wooden leg." Truth is often flawed and imperfect. What, indeed, is truth?

In 1943, Great Britain was planning an invasion of Sicily. In order to ensure the secrecy of this plan, the British military came up with an elaborate scheme to divert the attention of the Germans and Italians away from the intended invasion site. They found a corpse, endowed him with the fictitious name of Major William Martin, and planted fake papers in his uniform, including love letters from his fiancé. Also included were phony documents intended for the British commander in North Africa outlining a proposed invasion in Greece or Sardinia. The corpse was taken by submarine and dropped off the coast of Spain, where Spanish spies forwarded the documents to the German high command. The Germans were convinced and immediately diverted reinforcements to Greece and Sardinia. This helped to guarantee a successful Allied invasion of Sicily.[1]

It was an elaborate plan, but all the pieces fell into place and it worked. Most of the great achievements of human endeavor begin with a plan. According to the Epistle to the Ephesians (1:10), God has a "plan for the fullness of time" in which God is accomplishing "all things according to his counsel and will." There is a purpose to the universe.

Southern California mystery novelist and newspaper columnist T. Jefferson Parker focuses on the meaning of life in one of his columns. He recounts the true story of a local teenager who was convicted of killing his friend over a robbery dispute. The convicted murderer, Robert Chan, "wrote in letters to the court that he had read Albert Camus's book, *The Stranger*, some nine months before the murder and claimed that the book encouraged him to kill his victim because 'everything (is) meaningless and nothing matters because we are all going to die.'" Parker notes that he had read the same book some twenty years earlier when he was a teenager, but responded differently: "Rereading Chan's words," Parker writes, ". . . I was struck by how close he was to the mark, and at the same time how far away. Because we are all going to die, he reasons, everything is meaningless and nothing matters. But the truth is: Because we are all going to die nothing is meaningless and everything matters."[2] What is the ultimate purpose of the universe? What is the meaning of life? What is the truth of our existence?

I don't suppose these are the kinds of questions that come to mind while you are doing the dishes or mowing the lawn. And I must confess that I don't always ponder the mystery of life as I engage in the daily routines of ministry. However, there was one week that I did think about it a lot. It's not that what I did was all that unusual, but the events of each day led me to ponder the truth of existence and why we live out the experiences of our days.

On Monday, I drove two German visitors to Lancaster to visit a relative and a friend who were involved in an automobile accident. I thought of what it meant that they should come to this country to share for a week a bit of their German culture only to have this unfortunate and near-fatal

1. Montagu, *Man Who Never Was*.
2. Passantino, "Discovering God through Stories."

incident. And yet how much more we learned about each other and how much closer we all became because of it. The effect may ripple through time in both countries and produce future repercussions that we can know nothing about.

On Tuesday, I received a call from a young man in his twenties who was contemplating suicide because he was having difficulty facing his situation and could not see his way out of the dark tunnel he was in. Sometimes crises have a way of overpowering us so that we can't see beyond them. We lose hope because we can't see the longer view. We look where our feet are standing and fail to see the stars that lead to other possibilities and other opportunities. Because we can't see the future doesn't mean that there isn't any. Sometimes we have to trust that there is a purpose to existence and to our own life in particular.

On Wednesday, I attended a memorial service for Barbara Stratton, the widow of our college president. They had been members of my congregation. As the ushers were bringing in more chairs to accommodate the large number of friends and colleagues that attended, I thought of the rich legacy that this remarkable woman had left her community and the many lives she had touched through her various endeavors. And yet she lived only 66 years compared to her 101-year-old father, who was present with the rest of his family. It caused me to reflect that it is not the brevity of life that we should focus on, but the quality of it.

Sometimes it is important that we make waves, for we never know what distant shores they may reach. A hundred years from now, who will know that we have ever lived. We will be just one more stone in the cemetery. But you better believe that each of us will have made a difference in that world that is yet to be.

On Thursday, another man close to forty asked to speak with me. He had had a precognitive dream of a fire that occurred within a week, and he was becoming aware of a spiritual dimension in his life that had been largely ignored in the past. Having been raised with deep religious convictions, he was now experiencing and interpreting events that seemed to be in conflict with all he had been led to believe. We explored this together and he has now embarked on his own voyage of discovery of what this new awareness may mean for his own life.

Dr. Ellery Haskell, chair of the Department of History and Philosophy at Albright College, was a good friend. He gave me a copy of a book he recommended: *The Hidden Heart of the Cosmos* by Brian Swimme. Ellery and

I had been fellow travelers on the same spiritual paths for the past twenty-five years and when he recommends a book, I usually try to read it as soon as possible. This book on cosmology begins with the point that scientists have now discovered the birthplace of the universe, some fifteen billion light-years from earth. My first reaction was, "So what? Are they planning to put up a historical marker on the spot?" It's like having a photo of the Milky Way galaxy with a directional arrow indicating, "You Are Here." It seems totally irrelevant.

But as Brian Swimme points out, in an expanding universe, every point is moving away from every other point, and therefore every galaxy, every star, every planet is the center of the universe. Indeed, each one of us is the center of the universe, possessing a part of the consciousness of God.

As we explore the Martian landscape and extend our consciousness beyond the biosphere of this planet, we continue our search for extraterrestrial intelligence. The Mars rover Sojourner's cameras scan the horizon at Ares Vallis and we conclude that we are still alone in the universe. What did we expect—a McDonald's and a "Welcome to Mars" sign?

In a Kudzu comic strip, the preacher is sitting along the riverbank with a young parishioner. The young man says, "Preacher, why do so many people believe in extraterrestrials?"

The preacher answers, "Lonely, I reckon . . . They want desperately to believe there's somebody else out there so they won't feel so alone . . . They are probably disappointed in their fellow human beings!"

The young man asks, "But what if there is somebody out there?"

The preacher answers, "They'll be disappointed in us, too!" The preacher is probably right.

The search for the fulfillment of human destiny may take us to the infinite reaches of the universe, but if Einstein is right, that journey will lead right back to where we all began—in the mind of God.

When we realize that life is more than the accumulation of things, more than the pursuit of the transitory glories of the world, more than the feeding of our own egos with the approval of friends and colleagues; when we realize that the purpose of life is the journey of self-discovery that is found in the awareness of God's presence in the human soul, then we will have become conscious participants in the fulfill of God's plan. Then we will know the meaning of truth.

You may phrase it in whatever language you prefer: the salvation of your eternal soul by the acceptance of Jesus Christ as your personal Lord and Savior; or the recognition that there is a Supreme Being who has created you and cares for you and will ultimately gather you along with the physical and spiritual universe to himself; or that the Spirit that was in Jesus of Nazareth and was revealed through the life and teachings, death and resurrection of this man also abides in those who believe him and will by faith enable them to transcend their physical life to attain a different and better life in a spiritual existence. Various peoples in different ages and places have used different language to express the same eternal truth: God is in control of the universe and the universe is unfolding as it should. God has a plan for the fullness of time and that plan is in process. We all have a role in God's plan and we need to discover and accept the reason for our own being.

This is our hope and our faith. God has created us for a purpose: As it is written:

> he has made known to us the mystery of his will, according to his good pleasure that he set forth in Christ, as a plan for the fullness of time, to gather up all things in him, things in heaven and things on earth. In Christ we have also obtained an inheritance, having been destined according to the purpose of him who accomplishes all things according to his counsel and will, so that we, who were the first to set our hope on Christ, might live for the praise of his glory. (Ephesians 1:9–12)

The Bag Lady and the Transient

In our excessively busy lives, we move quickly through the routines of our day, often paying little attention to the people who cross our paths. In a time when we are confronted with signs that say "Black Lives Matter," or decry the latent prejudices against LGBTQ and varying ethnic groups in our society, we have become insensitive to persons who are different from us.

I once conducted an experiment on awareness, sensitivity, and caring in the church I was serving as pastor. St. John's United Church of Christ in the university town of Kutztown, Pennsylvania drew many visitors, many attracted to the wide variety of unique programs and worship experiences that I was offering. We were traditional and new age; we were eclectic and bizarre; we attracted students and persons from all faiths and no faith. In the process, it seemed that our regular church members might be ignoring those who might have special needs and were looking for help in some way.

On three successive Sundays, I arranged for two unusual visitors to attend Sunday worship. One was a transient whose scruffy, unshaven, and unkempt appearance set him apart from the other, well-dressed worshippers. The other was a "bag" clothed from head to toe in brown burlap with huge eyes, which Mary Ann had constructed and which I had persuaded a friend to wear.

The homeless person was Terry Lieb, director of Family Life Services at the Lutheran Home at Topton. Terry was accustomed to playing characters that might be unrecognizable. In an earlier incarnation he had been a clown with the Ringling Bros. Circus.

The bag attended a worship service in February 1984 and was met with some resistance by an usher who wasn't sure that it should be permitted to be seated. What if it were a terrorist in disguise carrying a concealed weapon? The bag did not speak during its first visit. On the following Sunday, I invited the bag to read the Scriptures. The congregation now knew that the bag was a woman.

The transient and bag visitations were designed to see how the congregation would respond to that which was strange and different, to see a person from whom we could not get visual feedback, who is a child of God, even though his or her appearance may be different from ours. After their solo appearances, I asked both to return on the following Sunday and to reflect upon the congregation's reaction.

Terry said, "I would be lying to say everyone greeted me with a big smile, but I felt a lot of warmth." "I sat down beside an elderly woman whom I immediately expected not to accept me," he said. "But to my surprise, she helped me with the hymnal, explained the service to me, and made sure that the Eucharist was offered to me." Later the woman gave him money to buy something to eat.

During the social time after the service, one couple invited the disheveled transient to their home for dinner. In his disguise as a stranger, Terry said he became aware of the part parents play as examples to their children, who look to them for cues on how to react.

"I saw young people watching, wondering how adults were going to respond to this stranger. This is an awesome responsibility for parents," he said. "How we reach out to strangers will affect how our young people do."

When the bag lady, whom I never identified, spoke, she said, "When the idea to go to church in a bag was first presented to me, it sounded far-out weird." But she liked the lesson for which it was intended. "It is perhaps within the realm of possibility that God can use a strange situation like this to show us how we respond to other people," she said.

Knees trembling and hands shaking, she felt fear the first time she came to the church—fear of being foolish and fear of being rejected, One woman shared her hymnal with the bag and at the end of the service said, "Please come again." That woman's kindness calmed the fear that the bag felt.

The bag lady said she learned that it was easy to hide behind the bag and to become dangerously comfortable with the distance it allows between people. "Do I hide behind bags in my regular daily life to keep me from letting others know who I am and from letting me know who they are?"

After the service, many children gathered around the bag, some braver than others, urging those who still had doubts to shake her hand. "C'mon, Kelly, it's OK. Don't be afraid," one girl told another.

One young teenager said. "I just thought that if a person like that wants to come to church, she should be welcomed. It doesn't matter how the person dresses."

One woman, who said she was a teacher and "acceptable to weird things," said that she thought the bag was "some sort of derelict with a gun underneath." She said she almost walked out of church when I asked the bag to read the Scriptures. "That angered me that he would allow someone to go to the pulpit and read the Scriptures dressed like that."

In the course of my long tenure at St. John's, we did many things that members and others thought crazy or weird, but the message seemed to have gotten through. After all, Jesus did some unusual and unexpected things that were peculiar and even countercultural, but his message has resonated down through the centuries.

Sensitivity to and awareness of the needs of other people became a top priority at the church, for the stranger in our midst is the Christ among us (Matthew 25).[1]

---

1. Debbie Garlicki reported on the event for the Allentown, Pennsylvania *Morning Call* (March 5, 1984) in an article entitled "Lesson of Love in Bag of Tricks Church Finds Clothes Don't Make the Man (or Woman)."

The Last Bell

It was close to midnight when Joyce Coleman called. Her neighbor, Florence Fisher, was very sick and wanted to see me. It was only a short trip up US-611, so I quickly got in the car and was there in a matter of minutes. Joyce and her husband, Les, were waiting for me on the front steps.

Florence was a retired schoolteacher, well into her eighties, and a faithful member of Mt. Zion Church. She had taught Sunday school for many years and worked tirelessly on behalf of the church. She became an elementary school teacher at a time when it was expected that those women entering the profession would take a vow of poverty and celibacy. In my ministry I would meet several of these dedicated women who virtually sacrificed any thought of a family of their own, but gave their lives to their profession. Many of them served in rural one-room schools throughout eastern Pennsylvania.

At the funeral of one of these gracious ladies, a mourner said to me before the service, "She was so good with the children. It's too bad that she had none of her own." And I would think of those final lines from James Hilton's *Goodbye, Mr. Chips*, when the dying Mr. Chipping says, "But you're wrong . . . I have thousands of them . . ." Florence had educated thousands and they were all her children.

But on this night she was alone and dying. We entered the old frame house that had been built in the previous century by her father. The living room had become a bedroom since Florence had grown too feeble to climb the steps. The one lamp on an end table pushed into the shadows the clutter of poverty and memory. Unlike those who are wealthy and can satisfy their needs immediately, the poor often hold on to everything, for many have been raised by frugal parents who taught them that you never know when you might need something. In Florence's home, however, was not so much the evidence of materialism, but the dusty debris of learning. Books were scattered about. Magazines and journals were opened to articles not yet read. Handwritten notes were on a pile of unopened mail.

The signs of sickness were also present. Prescription medication, patent medicine palliatives, crumpled tissues, and a dirty glass half filled with water lay amidst the magazines on the coffee table. The sofa was now her bed, and Florence had not moved from it in days. The odor in the room was the stench of death. It was the smell of decomposing flesh even as the spirit held tenaciously to the living body. I knew that Florence was dying.

"Thank you for coming, Pastor. I'm very sick. I would like you to pray for me and give me Communion."

The prayers I could offer, but I had left in such a hurry that I did not think to bring my Communion kit. I moved the wooden rocker alongside the sofa and sat down. Joyce had returned home, but I had asked Les to remain. He was an elder of the church and I needed him there. I talked briefly with Florence and then offered a prayer for her recovery. As soon as I said the "Amen," Florence opened her eyes and said, "Thank you, Pastor, but I am not going to get better. Will you give me Communion?"

I looked at Les, and then said to Florence, "Of course. Do you have any bread and wine?"

"No, I don't think so."

"Well, we'll find something." There was a box of saltine crackers on the end table. I went to the refrigerator. It was empty except for some condiments, butter, a couple of pieces of old fruit, and a small jar of prune juice. It would have to do. Les found three shot glasses in the cupboard.

For a young pastor just two years out of seminary, I was surprised at how many of the words I remembered. But it didn't matter. I broke the cracker and gave it to her. "This is my body."

I held up the small glass of prune juice. "This is my blood." We had Communion and Christ was there in our midst.

Florence died the next morning.

Ministry is not always what is said or what is done. Sometimes it is simply the gift of presence. When the wife of a good friend walked out on him and he was devastated, a group of us sat with him at Rocco's Bar. The elements of Communion were beer and pretzels. It didn't matter so much what we said, but just the fact that we were with him was encouraging and healing. It was a ministry of presence.

The sacrament of Holy Communion has always been very important for me because it represents the presence of Christ in the mystery of ritual. But Christ is just as real and just as present at those times and places when we need him most.

Being There

One of the most difficult and painful things a pastor is called upon to do is to break the news to a member of the parish that someone close to them has died. I have had to do that on several occasions and it has never been easy.

I was pastor of a church in Womelsdorf, Pennsylvania when an Air Force officer came to the parsonage and asked me to accompany him to the home of one of my older members. His job was to inform this seventy-two year-old man that his son, a career Air Force officer, was missing in action after his helicopter was hit by hostile fire over the Mekong Delta. We were admitted to Bob's house by his housekeeper. Twenty minutes later, Bob came in, carrying a bag of groceries. He saw the lieutenant in his uniform and me in clerics. Without saying a word, he put the groceries down on the kitchen counter and walked over and sat in his rocking chair by the window. He knew immediately why we were there.

The officer said something that sounded perfunctory and official, gave what details he could, and then said that he would be in touch. I sat with Bob for a long time in silence, knowing that I could not fully answer the unspoken question, "Why?" The year before, his wife had died of cancer. I knew that he had lived a rough life, and this was the ultimate crushing blow. I thought of Job, who had suffered one affliction after another and who still trusted in God. There was nothing I could say. And so we sat for awhile in silence; all I could do was be there—and it was enough.

When I went downstairs, the lieutenant was waiting to drive me back. We talked a little about Bob's situation, and then about his job. How did he feel about having to go to people's homes and tell them that their husband or son or father had been killed, that the person would never be coming through that door again?

What happens after the messengers have said those words can be hellish. And they can never know what will happen. Sometimes they find that they are the sole source of emotional support and comfort of the person being told. And that can be a difficult, painful role to play with a stranger. Sometimes they even fear for their own lives because disbelief can turn to violence. Nearly always there is blame, and sometimes the blame is turned on them and, again, they may be faced with violence.

I had heard from a friend who was raised in Syria that there it was a custom that when a death occurred, friends and family would gather with the bereaved. They would sit together in silence. No words were spoken. They would explore together the meaning of the event. It was in the silence, simply being present, that one found comfort.

I sat at the bedside of a woman whose memory was failing and whose mind could not grasp the awareness of her environment. I had entered her room at the nursing facility where she was living and saw that she was sleeping, and so I sat down as I waited in silence for her to wake from her nap. After a few minutes, she opened her eyes and noted my presence, but did not realize that it was her pastor that came to visit. She simply said, "I love you."

How typical of a woman who loved so much that she gave her life in service to others. Her mental abilities were diminishing even as her aged body curled within the warmth of her blanket. Her body and her mind were no longer what they had been, but her soul still reflected the essence of her being—that of love.

Johannes Eckhart of Hochheim, the great German mystic and theologian, once said, "If the only prayer you ever say in your entire life is 'thank you,' it will be enough. But to say 'I love you' to every person you meet, whether or not you recognize them, speaks from the very heart of God."

When I was a child of seven or eight, my greatest desire was for a set of Lionel trains. When Christmas would come around, my friends and I would always go to the window at Macy's and watch their elaborate setup. Some of the kids had trains in their basement and they would talk about what accessories they were going to get for Christmas that year. But my folks couldn't afford it. It wasn't until I was fourteen years old that my father gave me a train set for Christmas. By that time I was no longer interested in trains. I was looking forward to a car.

I still put that old set under the Christmas tree each year as a reminder of how our values change; how what is most important in our lives at one stage of our lives loses its luster when we have attained it; how prayers once uttered and forgotten eventually come back to us, sometimes as a blessing. But sometimes we are blessed by unanswered prayer.

God knows what is in our hearts and what our desires are. God doesn't need our words as much as we need to speak them. Now when I look under our Christmas tree and see the words on the side of that train set, it has a different meaning. "Lionel." Lion—the most powerful of animals. *El*—the ancient Hebrew word for God. Our God is a God of power who hears our unspoken prayers and intercedes for us with sighs too deep for words.

In the times of our greatest crises, when we are in the midst of despair and we do not hear the voice of God's comfort, it is enough to know that God is present.

Elie Wiesel, in his memoir *Night*, tells of seeing a young boy dying a slow death on the gallows at Birkenau, a victim of the Holocaust. He heard a man ask, "'For God's sake, where is God?' And from within me, I heard a voice answer: 'Where is He? This is where—hanging here from this gallows . . .'"[1]

The mystical moment is any moment when we become aware of the presence of God, whether it is a moment of ecstasy, an act of empathy and compassion, or a time of deep tragedy and despair.

---

1. Wiesel, *Night*, 65.

Pou Sto

I continue to remember the young man who was the youth leader of the congregation that I served. He was not only one of my parishioners, but a friend. We worked out together at the health spa, took our youth on retreats, discussed religion and philosophy. He confided in me when he wrestled with decisions when he fell in love with a married woman. He had trouble seeing anything positive in the political and social events of the times. However, he was very careful not to let his internal struggles affect his relationship with the youth and other members of the congregation. They had no idea what he was struggling with.

On the day before Christmas, he drove to the town park, put a shotgun between his legs, and pulled the trigger. It was one of the most difficult Christmas Eve services that I have ever had to conduct. With what was going on in the world at the time—Vietnam, environmental destruction, the Cold War—he felt he was living in the last days of planet Earth, and in his depression could not bear it, and so he took his own life. What he could never know was that it was the world inside, not the world outside, that led to his decision. His depression shaped his perception of reality, which in turn reinforced his depression—a downward spiral into madness and self-destruction.

We must not only be careful how we look at life, but we must also examine the lenses through which we see our world. Our mental and spiritual health depends upon it.

Following the terrorist attacks of September 11, this prayer was found:

> O God, open all doors to me. O God, who answers prayers, I'm asking for your help. I'm asking you for forgiveness. I'm asking you to lighten my way. I'm asking you to lift the burden. O God, you who opens all doors, open all doors for me. Open all venues to me. Open all avenues for me. God, I trust in you. God I lay myself in your hands. There is no God but God. We are of God, and to God we return.

It is a prayer that we might pray, but it was written by Mohammad Atta, the apparent ringleader of the terrorists. How does God hear the prayers of Muslims, Jews, and Christians?

Of this I am certain: God is far beyond our perception of God and we must still struggle to interpret God's intention for human life. But it is the nature of evil and of diseased minds to take what is basically good and twist it to demonic purposes. For centuries we have seen so much evil in this world perpetrated in the name of religion, but it is all an aberration of the principles of true faith. Where we stand determines what we see. Our experiences, our culture, our education—so many factors—shape and guide our perceptions, and we see the world through those lenses.

Archimedes of Syracuse, the ancient Greek mathematician and physicist, once said, "Give me a place to stand and I will move the earth." He was referring to using a fulcrum in exerting leverage in moving large objects. However, his term *pou sto* literally means a standing place or vantage point. Who we are, what we have learned, where we live, with whom we associate, and so many other factors determine how we interpret the world and how we react to it.

In the siege of Syracuse, Archimedes was killed by a Roman soldier, contrary to the orders of the Proconsul Marcellus, who was enraged when the mathematician told him he needed to finish the problem he was working on.

Science, politics, and religion must often contend with the forces of ignorance, but in the penultimate we shall all stand in the right place at the judgment seat of God.

We are living between the no longer and the not yet, a transitional period between this world and the next. We may indeed be running out of time. But time is relative, and in the mind of God time does not exist. From where God stands, past, present, and future are but a moment, a twinkling of the eye. Perhaps Jesus is right. As the destruction of Jerusalem by the Romans in 70 AD was the beginning of a new age, so the groaning and travail of these times are the birth pangs of a new creation, a necessary period that we must endure in order to bring forth a new and better world. For God is "about to create new heavens and a new earth; the former things shall not be remembered or come to mind" (Isaiah 65:17). Let us be aware of where we stand.

Tell Me Your Story

There is a song by Glyn Lehmann that begins, "Tell me your story; we all have a story to tell," and then we become a part of one another's story.

When I was a small child, my grandmother would take me shopping uptown in the city's commercial and business area. At one particular street corner, near a public fountain, there was a blind man who had two cups. One was filled with pencils and the other wasn't. The idea was that passersby would take a pencil from the one cup and put a nickel in the other. Some people would drop coins in his cup without taking a pencil; others would put in a penny and try to take more than one pencil. The blind man always knew. But he always offered a blessing—even to those who took advantage of him.

Over the years that I was growing up, I would see him there on hot summer days and cold winter evenings. I remember thinking at one time, "I wonder how he gets to that corner every day. Who supplies his pencils? Is he married? Where does he live? What is his life like, spending all that time at that one corner?" I guess I was a high school senior when I first realized he wasn't there any longer. I never gave him another thought until many years later. After all, he was simply a face in the crowd, a familiar stranger whom you know, but never really know.

There is often an untold story in each person. As a ninth-grader sitting in a doctor's waiting room that was empty except for the receptionist, I had some anxiety about my appointment. The young woman would look up occasionally and cast a reassuring smile, but we said very little except that which was necessary. And then the phone rang. She answered in her usual pleasant voice, but then a moment later her expression dramatically changed. Tears came quickly as she hung up the phone, put her head on the desk, and sobbed uncontrollably. She arose, left the room through the doctor's office, and I never saw her again. On my next visit there was a new receptionist.

I never asked, but always wondered, what had happened. Would it have made a difference in my life if I had known the details of the incident? Was there anything that I could have said to comfort someone I barely knew?

Every person has a story to tell, but we are strangers to one another because we do not take the time to listen, or even to ask. It is not a matter of being intrusive, but of caring for another.

During my first week in Jerusalem at Christ Church Hospice, I met a Dutchman, the real kind from the Netherlands, at a cafe run by a Palestinian Christian. This Dutchman had lived in Jerusalem for several years and we got to talking about the art of the deal when visiting the souks in the Old City. He gave me some helpful bits of advice.

"Always wear sunglasses when shopping," he said. "These Arabs look at your eyes because your pupils tend to dilate when they come across something you really like. They also can tell when you have arrived at the price you are willing to pay. And don't tell a shopkeeper that you will think about something and come back, because if they see you in the street later on, they will come after you and hold you to your promise. But most important of all, if you are out in the villages, never accept the first price that is offered to you. It is considered an insult because you are not taking the time to establish a relationship."

We saw this especially in Turkey when looking for a rug. There is a ritual that must be followed. You are first offered coffee or tea, which you must accept, and then you learn about the shopkeeper's family and he asks about yours, and then how you are enjoying your trip and how you like his country. Then you talk about the rugs and how they are made. Only after about thirty minutes do you begin discussing the price. You must first establish a relationship, a connection, so that you are no longer strangers to one another.

A good friend who was the dean of students at Kutztown University and I were talking about how the Internet was affecting the lives of students. While it has become a source of learning, an instant reference always at the tips of your fingers, the electronic relationships of emails and chat rooms were diminishing human contact. The interactions of conversation, eye contact, and body language were eroding. The world is becoming like the George Tooker painting of an infinite office complex where each person occupies his or her own Dilbert-like cubicle, except that there are no doors on the cubicles. We exist in isolation, and therefore we lose the collective wisdom that comes from a gathered community. Our connections to one another, our relationships, are so important. When we break those relationships, we become disconnected. That is why there is no such thing as a private spirituality.

Jean Paul Sartre, in his play *No Exit*, describes hell as other people, but it is people who are isolated from one another. If we can't get along with our neighbor in this world, what makes us think we are going to in the next? When you speak ill of another person, or give them the cold shoulder, or refuse to speak to someone, you add to the alienation that exists in this world, and you wound the heart of God, who binds us together in common love. It is our stories that unite us. We need to listen to each other to identify with our common humanity. It is by careful and empathetic listening that we enter into the soul of another, and in so doing find that the story we hear is also our story.

Joan Didion wrote a book of collected narratives with the title *We Tell Ourselves Stories in Order to Live*. Not only do our stories shape our own lives, but when we listen to the stories of others, we recognize that we are all part of a common consciousness. Each person's story is important to the one story of why humans exist.

We are created to be in relationship, to interact with our world. While it is important to take time to be alone from time to time, the true mystic who is aware of the presence of God always returns from the desert to be in community and to see God at work among all peoples.

Some of my ministerial colleagues occasionally complain about the seemingly endless schedule of meetings and events that they must attend. The work of the church is not only worship and Bible studies, but fellowship dinners, and youth dances, and art and music events, and, yes, a seeming interminable schedule of meetings, because they are precisely that—opportunities for people to meet each other and interact with one another. Only when we meet can we come to know each other intimately and become the body of Christ.

The path to wisdom is a common path, the gathering of many candles to produce a great light. Catherine of Sienna once said, "All the way to heaven is heaven." When we are together, when we enter into one another's story, when we find common grounds to love one another, then we grow wiser, and we grow hope for the world.

As Leo Joseph Cardinal Suenens once said, "It is in each of us that the peace of the world is cast . . . in the frontiers of our hearts. From there it must spread out to the limits of the universe."[1] That can happen when we tell one another our own stories.

---

1. Quoted at http://www.octanecreative.com/reinform/peace_thoughts.html.

Bibliography

Boissiere, Robert. *The Return of Pahana*. Santa Fe: Bear, 1990.
Borglum, David. "Honoring Our Mother: Cultivating a Spirituality of the Earth." *Spirit Unfolding* (newsletter of the Spiritual Development Network of the United Church of Christ), Spring 1997.
Clinebell, Howard. *Ecotherapy: Healing Ourselves, Healing the Earth*. Minneapolis: Fortress, 1996.
DeChant, Clement W. *Out of My Heart: A Pastor's Diary*. Philadelphia: Christian Education, 1952.
Einstein, Albert. "The World as I See It." In *Living Philosophies*, by Albert Einstein et al. New York: Simon and Schuster, 1931.
Frankl, Viktor E. *Man's Search for Meaning: An Introduction to Logotherapy*. Pocket Book edition. Boston: Beacon, 1959.
Gibran, Kahlil. *The Prophet*. New York: Knopf, 1923.
Gore, Albert, Jr. "The Story of the Earth and Us." In *Sacred Stories: A Celebration of the Power of Stories to Transform and Heal*, edited by Charles Simpkinson and Anne Simpkinson. San Francisco: Harper San Francisco, 1993.
Hopke, Robert H. *There Are No Accidents: Synchronicity and the Stories of Our Lives*. New York: Riverhead, 1997.
Kabat-Zinn, Jon. *Wherever You Go, There You Are: Mindfulness Meditation for Everyday Life*. New York: Hyperion, 1994.
Masson, Jeffrey Moussaieff, and Susan McCarthy. *When Elephants Weep: The Emotional Lives of Animals*. New York: Delta, 1996.
Montagu, Ewen. *The Man Who Never Was*. New York: Oxford University Press, 1953.
Passantino, Gretchen. "Discovering God through Stories." 2003. https://www.answers.org/issues/discovering_god_through_stories.html.
Pritchard, Evan T. *No Word for Time: The Way of the Algonquin People*. Graham, NC: Millichap, 1997.
Untermeyer, Louis. *A Treasury of Great Poems, English and American*. New York: Simon and Schuster, 1942.
Wiesel, Elie. *Night*. New York: Hill and Wang, 1958.
Wolfe, Thomas. *Look Homeward, Angel*. New York: Scribner, 1929.
———. *You Can't Go Home Again*. New York: Scribner, 1934.

www.ingramcontent.com/pod-product-compliance
Lightning Source LLC
Chambersburg PA
CBHW071431160426
43195CB00013B/1871